To Kill a Mockingbird:
The Screenplay

and Related Readings

McDougal Littell
A HOUGHTON MIFFLIN COMPANY

Evanston, Illinois *Boston* *Dallas*

Acknowledgments

Simon & Schuster: Excerpt from *Growing Up in the Great Depression* by Richard Wormser; Copyright © 1994 by Richard Wormser. Reprinted by permission of Atheneum Books for Younger Readers, an imprint of Simon & Schuster.
George Garrett: "The Right Thing to Do," from *The Sound of Writing* by George Garrett. Reprinted by permission of the author.
Music Sales Corporation and Carlin America, Inc.: "Strange Fruit" by Lewis Allan; Copyright 1939 by Edward B. Marks Corporation. Renewed © by Music Sales Corporation (ASCAP) and Edward B. Marks Corporation. Reprinted by permission of Music Sales Corporation and by permission of Edward B. Marks Corporation, a division of Carlin America, Inc. All rights reserved.

Continued on page 137.

The editors have made every effort to trace the ownership of all copyrighted selections found in this book and to make full acknowledgment for their use. Omissions brought to our attention will be corrected in a subsequent edition.

To Kill a Mockingbird screenplay by Horton Foote, Copyright © 1964 by Boardwalk Productions and Brentwood Productions, Inc. Reprinted by permission of Barbara Hogenson Literary Agency and McIntosh & Otis, Inc.
WARNING:
This screenplay is not to be performed either by professionals or amateurs. The amateur and stock rights to *To Kill a Mockingbird* (dramatized by Christopher Sergel) are controlled by The Dramatic Publishing Company, P.O. Box 109, Woodstock, IL 60098.

Cover illustration by John Ferry.
Author photo (Horton Foote): AP/Wide World Photos.

ISBN 0-395-79678-4

4567—DCI—02 01 00 99 98

Contents

Continued

To Kill a Mockingbird:
The Screenplay

Horton Foote

Cast of Characters

Atticus Finch

Scout Finch

Jem Finch

Dill Harris

Sheriff Heck Tate

Miss Maudie Atkinson

Mrs. Dubose

Tom Robinson

Calpurnia

Judge Taylor

Mayella Ewell

Bob Ewell

Stephanie Crawford

Boo Radley

Gilmer

Walter Cunningham

Mr. Radley

Walter Cunningham, Jr.

Reverend Sykes

Narration (Jean Louise Finch)

FADE IN. EXTERIOR: MAYCOMB, ALABAMA. DAYBREAK.

> *It is just before dawn, and in the half-light*
> *cotton farms, pinewoods, the hills*
> *surrounding Maycomb, and the*
> *Courthouse Square are seen. A young*
> *woman's voice is heard.*

Jean Louise (*voice over*). Maycomb was a tired old town, even in 1932 . . . when I first knew it. Somehow, it was hotter then. Men's stiff collars wilted by nine in the morning. Ladies bathed before noon and after their three o'clock naps. And by nightfall they were like soft teacakes with frosting from sweating and sweet talcum. The day was twenty-four hours long, but it seemed longer. There's no hurry, for there's nowhere to go and nothing to buy . . . and no money to buy it with. Although Maycomb County had recently been told that it had nothing to fear but fear itself.

(*The Finch house and yard are seen. It is a small frame house, built high off the ground and with a porch in the manner of Southern cottages of its day. The yard is a large one, filled with oaks, and it has an air of mystery about it in the early morning light.*)

That summer, I was six years old.

(Walter Cunningham, *a thin, raw-boned farmer in his late fifties, comes into view. He is carrying a crokersack full of hickory nuts. He passes under the oak tree at the side of the house. Scout, six, dressed in blue jeans, drops from one of its branches to the ground. She brushes herself off and goes toward* Mr. Cunningham.)

Scout. Good morning, Mr. Cunningham.

Cunningham. Mornin' Miss.

Scout. My daddy is getting dressed. Would you like me to call him for you?

Cunningham. No, Miss . . . I . . . don't care to bother.

Scout. Why, it's no bother, Mr. Cunningham. He'll be happy to see you. Atticus. (Scout *hurries up the steps and opens the door.*) Atticus, here's Mr. Cunningham.

(Scout *steps back onto the porch as* Atticus *enters.* Walter Cunningham *seems ill at ease and embarrassed.*)

Atticus. Good morning, Walter.

Cunningham. Good morning, Mr. Finch. I . . . didn't want to bother you none. I brung you these hickory nuts as part of my entailment.

Atticus (*reaching for the sack of nuts*). Well, I thank you. The collards we had last week were delicious.

Cunningham (*gesturing, and then turning to leave*). Well, good morning.

Atticus. Good morning, Walter.

(Atticus *holds the sack of nuts.* Scout *is on the steps behind him.* Scout *leans on* Atticus' *shoulders as they watch* Mr. Cunningham *leave.*)

Scout, I think maybe next time Mr. Cunningham comes, you better not call me.

Scout. Well, I thought you'd want to thank him.

Atticus. Oh, I do. I think it embarrasses him to be thanked.

(Atticus *turns and puts the sack on the porch and starts for the front yard to get the morning papers.* Scout *follows after him.*)

Scout. Why does he bring you all this stuff?

Atticus. He is paying me for some legal work I did for him.

Scout. Why is he paying you like this?

Atticus. That's the only way he can . . . he has no money.

(Atticus *comes back to the porch as* Scout *follows. He picks up the newspaper and reads.*)

Scout. Is he poor?

Atticus. Yes.

Scout. Are we poor?

Atticus. We are indeed.

Scout. Are we as poor as the Cunninghams?

Atticus. No, not exactly. The Cunninghams are country folks, farmers, and the crash hit them the hardest.

(Calpurnia, *in her late fifties, appears at the screen door.*)

Calpurnia. Scout, call your brother. (*She goes back inside.*)

Scout. Atticus, Jem is up in the tree. He says he won't come down until you agree to play football for the Methodists.

(Atticus *walks toward the tree. In a treehouse, high up in the tree, sits* Jem. *He is ten, with a serious, manly little face. Right now, he is scowling.*)

Atticus. Jem . . . Son, why don't you come on down and have your breakfast? Calpurnia has a good one . . . hot biscuits.

Jem. No Sir. Not until you agree to play football for the Methodists.

(Atticus *is looking up at* Jem. Scout *is swinging in the tire swing.*)

Atticus. Oh, no, Son. I can't do that. I explained to you I'm too old to get out there. After all, I'm the only father you have. You wouldn't want me to get out there and get my head knocked off, would you?

Jem. I ain't coming down.

Atticus. Suit yourself.

(Atticus *turns and starts for the kitchen door as he reads the newspaper.* Jem *moves out from behind the covering and watches.* Scout *starts to go across the street and stops by the tree.* Miss Maudie Atkinson, *a strong, warm-hearted woman, keenly interested in* Atticus *and the children, is working on her flowers in her yard across the street.*)

Maudie. Good morning.

Scout. Good morning, Miss Maudie.

Maudie. What's going on over there?

Scout. I'm having a terrible time, Miss Maudie. Jem is staying up in that tree until Atticus agrees to play football for the Methodists, and Atticus says he's too old.

Jem. Every time I want him to do something . . . he's too old . . . He's too old for anything.

Maudie. He can do plenty of things.

Atticus (*entering the yard from the house and walking over*). You be good, children, and mind Cal. Good morning, Maudie.

Maudie. Good morning, Atticus.

(*Church bells ring.*)

Jem. He won't let me have a gun. He'll only play touch football with me . . . never tackle.

Maudie (*glancing in* Atticus' *direction, then looking at* Jem). He can make somebody's will so airtight you can't break it. You count your blessings and stop complaining . . . both of you.

(Atticus *continues on out of the yard.* Miss Maudie *walks away.* Scout *climbs up into the tree.*)

Scout. Jem, he is pretty old.

Jem. I can't help that.

(*He swings down to the lower limb in disgust and looks down into Miss Stephanie Crawford's collard patch next door. A boy,* Dill, *is sitting among the collards. Sitting down, he is not much higher than the collards. He has a solemn, owlish face, a knowledge and imagination too old for his years. He looks up at* Jem.)

Dill (*tentatively*). Hey . . .

Jem. Hey, yourself.

Dill (*standing up*). I'm Charles Baker Harris. I can read. You got anything needs reading, I can do it.

Jem. How old are you? Four and a half?

Dill. Going on seven.

Jem. Well, no wonder then. Scout's been reading since she was born and don't start to school till next month. You look right puny for goin' on seven.

Dill. I'm little, but I'm old. Folks call me Dill. I'm from Meridian, Mississippi, and I'm spending two weeks next door with my Aunt Stephanie. My mama works for a photographer in Meridian. She entered my picture in the "Beautiful Child Contest" and won five dollars. She gave the money to me and I went to the picture show twenty times with it.

(Scout *and* Jem *climb down from the treehouse.* Scout *climbs into the tire swing as* Jem *leans against the tree facing* Dill.)

Scout. Our mama's dead, but we got a daddy. Where's your daddy?

Dill. I haven't got one.

Scout. Is he dead?

Dill. No.

Scout. Well . . . if he's not dead, you've got one, haven't you?

(Jem *turns to* Scout.)

Jem. Hush, Scout.

(Jem *motions to her with his head as* Scout *whispers.*)

Scout. What's happened, what's up?

(Calpurnia *enters with a shirt, and starts to dress* Scout.)

Dill, this is Calpurnia.

Calpurnia. Pleased to know you, Dill.

Dill. Pleased to know you. My daddy owns the L and N Railroad. He's going to let me run the engine all the way to New Orleans.

Calpurnia. Is that so?

(Calpurnia *exits.* Jem *turns away.* Scout *finishes putting on her shirt.*)

Dill. He says I can invite . . . anybody . . .

Jem. Shhh!

(Mr. Radley, *in his seventies, a regal, austere man, walks by.* Scout *and* Jem *see him and become very subdued, as if they were afraid. Their attention leaves* Dill, *and he senses this and looks at them to see what is happening.*)

There goes the meanest man that ever took a breath of life.

Dill. Why is he the meanest man?

Jem. Well, for one thing he has a boy named Boo that he keeps chained to a bed in that house over yonder. (*Points to the house.*) See, he lives over there.

(*Moving shot. As they start to move out of the yard,* Scout *follows behind them. They go down the sidewalk past Miss Stephanie's house, north to the Radley house.*)

Boo only comes out at night when we are asleep and it's pitch-dark. When you wake up at night you can hear him. Once I heard him scratching on our screen door, but he was gone by the time Atticus got there.

(*They are standing by a light pole now, staring at the Radley house and yard. The house is low and was once white with a deep front porch and green shutters. But it darkened long ago to the color of the slate-gray yard around it. Rain-spotted shingles droop over the eaves of the veranda. Oak trees keep the sun away. The remains of a picket fence drunkenly guard the front yard. A "swept" yard that is never swept, where Johnson grass and rabbit tobacco grow in abundance. Dill's eyes have widened. He is becoming truly intrigued.*)

Dill. Wonder what he does in there?

Scout. I wonder what he looks like?

Jem. Well, judging from his tracks, he's about six and a half feet tall. He eats raw squirrels and all the cats he can catch. There's a long, jagged scar running all the way across his face. His teeth are yellow and rotten. His eyes are popped. And he drools most of the time.

Dill. Aw, I don't believe you.

(Miss Stephanie, Dill's *aunt, comes up behind them. She is in her late fifties—a spinster and the neighborhood gossip. She comes up without their hearing her. She has a habit of half-shouting when she talks.*)

Stephanie. Dill, what are you doing here?

Dill. My Lord, Aunt Stephanie, you almost gave me a heart attack.

Stephanie. Dill, I don't want you playing around that house over there. There's a maniac living there and he's dangerous.

Jem. See? I was just trying to warn him about Boo, and he wouldn't believe me.

Stephanie. Well, you'd just better believe him, Mr. Dill Harris.

Jem. Tell him about the time Boo tried to kill his papa.

Stephanie. Well, I was standing in my yard one day when his mama come out yelling, "He's killing us all." Turned out that Boo was sitting in the living room cutting up the paper for his scrapbook, and when his daddy come by, he reached over with his scissors, stabbed him in his leg, pulled them out, and went right on cutting the paper.

(Dill's *eyes are popping with excitement.*)

They wanted to send him to an asylum, but his daddy said no Radley was going to any asylum. So they locked him up in the basement of the courthouse till he nearly died of the damp, and his daddy brought him home. And there he is to this day, sittin' over there with his scissors . . . Lord knows what he's doin' or thinkin'.

EXTERIOR: FINCH YARD. DAY.

> Jem *is swinging in the tire swing. In the distance the town clock is heard to strike five.*

Jem. Come on, Scout, it's five o'clock. (*Jumps from the swinging tire and starts to run out of the yard.*)

Dill. Where you going?

Scout. It's time to meet Atticus.

(*She runs after* Jem; Dill *follows her.*)

(*Moving shot. They run down the street.*)

Dill. Why do you call your daddy "Atticus"?

Scout. 'Cause Jem does.

Dill. Why does he?

Scout. I don't know. He just started to when he began talking.

(*They run up the street toward town.* Jem *slows down.*)

Jem. Mrs. Dubose is on her porch. (*He gestures to* Dill.) Listen, no matter what she says to you, don't answer her back. There's a Confederate pistol in her lap under her shawl and she'll kill you quick as look at you. Come on.

(*They walk cautiously on and start to pass the Dubose house. It is an old and run-down house. It has steep front steps and a dogtrot hall.* Mrs. Henry Lafayette Dubose *sits on the front porch in her wheelchair. Beside her is a Negro girl,* Jessie, *who takes care of her.*)

Scout. Hey, Mrs. Dubose.

Mrs. Dubose (*snarling at the children*). Don't you say "hey" to me, you ugly girl. You say "good afternoon" to me. You come over here when I'm talking to you.

(Scout, Jem, *and* Dill *keep on going. They are made very uncomfortable by her. They see* Atticus *coming and run toward him.*)

Jem. Atticus, this is Dill. He's Miss Stephanie's nephew.

Atticus. How do you do, Dill.

Mrs. Dubose. Listen to me when I'm talking to you. Don't your daddy teach you to respect old people? You come back here, Jean Louise Finch . . .

Atticus (*taking the children and walking over to her porch*). Good afternoon, Mrs. Dubose. My, you look like a picture this afternoon.

(*The children are trying to hide behind* Atticus. *They begin to giggle nervously at each other.*)

Scout (*whispering*). He don't say a picture of what.

Atticus (*turning to look at the yard*). My goodness gracious, look at your flowers. Did you ever see anything more beautiful? (*He gestures with hand holding hat*). Mrs. Dubose, the gardens at Bellingrath have nothing to compare with your flowers.

Mrs. Dubose. Oh, I don't think they're as nice as last year.

Atticus. Oh, I can't agree with you.

Jem (*whispering*). He gets her interested in something nice, and she forgets to be mean.

(*The three children are standing behind* Atticus. Atticus *hits* Jem *with his hat.*)

Atticus. I think that your yard is going to be the showplace of the town.

(*The children giggle.*)

Well, grand seeing you, Mrs. Dubose.

(*He puts on his hat. They start on.*)

INTERIOR: SCOUT'S ROOM. NIGHT.

> *She is undressed and in bed.* Atticus *is seated on the bed.* Scout *is reading to him from* Robinson Crusoe.

Scout. "I had two cats which I brought ashore on my first raft, and I had a dog . . . " (*Holds the book to her face and looks at* Atticus.) Atticus, do you think Boo Radley ever comes and looks in my window at night? Jem says he does. This afternoon when we were over by their house . . .

Atticus (*interrupting*). Scout, I told you and Jem to leave those poor people alone. I want you to stay away from their house and stop tormenting them.

Scout. Yes Sir.

Atticus (*looking at his pocket watch*). Well, I think that's all the reading for tonight, honey . . . it's getting late.

(*She closes the book and he sits up and takes the book and puts it on the table.*)

Scout. What time is it?

Atticus. Eight-thirty.

Scout. May I see your watch?

(*He gives it to her. She opens the case and reads the inscription.*)

"To Atticus, my beloved husband." Atticus, Jem says this watch is going to belong to him some day.

Atticus. That's right.

Scout. Why?

Atticus. Well, it's customary for the boy to have his father's watch.

Scout. What are you going to give me?

Atticus. Well, I don't know that I have much else of value that belongs to me. But there's a pearl necklace . . . and there's a ring that belonged to your mother . . . and I've put them away . . . and they're to be yours.

(Scout *stretches her arms and smiles.* Atticus *kisses her cheek. He takes his watch and gets up. He covers her and puts out the lamp.*)

Good night, Scout.

Scout. Good night.

Atticus. Good night, Jem.

Jem (*from his room*). Good night.

(Atticus *goes out.*)

INTERIOR: JEM'S ROOM. NIGHT.

> Jem *pulls the covers over himself in the darkness.*

INTERIOR: SCOUT'S ROOM. NIGHT.

> Scout *lies in bed, thinking.*

Scout. Jem?

Jem (*off camera*). Yes?

Scout. How old was I when Mama died?

Jem (*off camera*). Two.

Scout. And how old were you?

Jem (*off camera*). Six.

Scout. Old as I am now?

Jem (*off camera*). Uh huh.

Scout. Was Mama pretty?

Jem (*off camera*). Uh huh.

EXTERIOR: FRONT PORCH. NIGHT.

> Atticus *is on the front porch. He can hear the children's conversation.*

Scout (*off camera*). Was Mama nice?

Jem (*off camera*). Uh huh.

Scout (*off camera*). Did you love her?

Jem (*off camera*). Yes.

Scout (*off camera*). Did I love her?

Jem (*off camera*). Yes.

Scout (*off camera*). Do you miss her?

Jem (*off camera*). Uh huh.

(*There is silence. Atticus listens to the night sounds.* Judge Taylor, *seventy-five, comes up on the porch.*)

Judge. Evening, Atticus.

Atticus. Evening, Judge.

(*The Judge walks over to him and pulls up a chair as he starts to sit.*)

Rather warm, isn't it?

Judge. Yes, indeed. (*Fans himself with his hat.*)

Atticus. How's Mrs. Taylor?

Judge. She's fine . . . fine. Thank you. (*A pause.*) Atticus, you heard about Tom Robinson?

Atticus. Yes Sir.

Judge. Grand jury will get around to chargin' him tomorrow. (*A pause.*) I was thinking about appointing you to take the case. Though I realize you're very busy these days with your practice. And your children need a great deal of your time.

Atticus. Yes Sir. (*Reflects thoughtfully.*) I'll take the case.

Judge. I'll send a boy for you tomorrow when his hearing comes up. (*The Judge rises.*) Well, I'll see you tomorrow, Atticus.

Atticus. Yes Sir.

Judge. And thank you.

Atticus. Yes Sir.

(Judge Taylor *leaves. Again there is silence.* Atticus *rocks and listens to the night sounds.*)

EXTERIOR: FINCH PORCH. THE NEXT MORNING.

>Jem, Dill, *and* Scout *enter through the door.* Dill *turns to Jem.*

Dill. Hey, Jem, I bet you a "Grey Ghost" against two "Tom Swifts," you won't go any farther than Boo Radley's gate.

Jem. Aw . . .

(*They start down the steps,* Jem *in the lead.*)

Dill. You're scared to, ain't you?

Jem. I ain't scared. I go past Boo Radley's house nearly every day of my life.

Scout. Always running.

(Jem *and* Dill *turn to her.* Jem *shoves her.*)

Jem. You hush up, Scout. (*Starts wheeling a rubber tire.*) Come on, Dill.

Scout. Me first, me first . . . me first.

(Jem *stops with the tire and turns to* Scout.)

Jem. You've gotta let Dill go first.

Scout (*jumping up and down angrily*). No, no, me first.

Dill. Oh, let her go.

Jem. Scout, be still. All right, get in.

(Jem *takes hold of the tire and* Scout *gets inside it.*)

Hurry up.

Scout. All right.

Jem. You ready?

Scout. Uh huh. Let her go.

(*When she is inside,* Jem *suddenly pushes it with all his might.*)

(*Moving shot. It leaves the sidewalk, goes across the gravel road to the sidewalk in front of the Radley place, through the gate, up the Radley sidewalk, hits the steps of the porch, and then rolls over on its side.* Dill *and* Jem *watch this with helpless terror.* Scout, *dizzy and nauseated, and unaware of where she is, lies on the ground.*)

Jem (*yelling frantically*). Scout, get away from there. Scout, come on.

(Scout *raises her head and sees where she is. She is frozen with terror.*)

Scout, don't just lie there. Get up!

(Jem *runs to* Scout, *seated on the ground in front of the house.*)

Let's go.

(*He gets his sister by the hand, then looks up at the house, drops her hand, runs up the steps to the front door, touches it, comes running down, grabs the tire, takes his sister by the hand, and starts running out of the yard.*)

Run for your life, Scout. Come on, Dill!

(*Moving shot. They run out of the yard, up the sidewalk to their own yard.* Dill *runs fast behind them. When they get to the safety of their yard, they are all exhausted and fall on the ground.* Jem *is elated by his feat of touching the Radley house.*)

Now who's a coward? You tell them about this back in Meridian County, Mr. Dill Harris.

(Dill *looks at* Jem *with new respect.*)

Dill. I'll tell you what let's do. Let's go down to the courthouse and see that room they locked Boo up in. My aunt says it's bat-infested, and he almost died from the mildew. Come on. I bet they got chains and instruments of torture down there. Come on!

(Dill *runs out of the yard, as* Jem *and* Scout *reluctantly follow.*)

EXTERIOR: COURTHOUSE SQUARE. DAY.

A group of four idlers sit lounging under some live oak trees. They watch with eagle eyes whatever happens on the square and in the courthouse.

Dill, *followed by* Scout *and* Jem, *come by them.*

One of the men, Hiram Townsend, *recognizes* Scout *and* Jem. *He is in his seventies and is dressed in work clothes.*

Hiram. Jem Finch?

Jem. Yes Sir.

Hiram. If you're looking for your daddy, he's inside the courthouse.

Scout. Thank you, Sir, but we're not looking for . . .

(Jem *gives her a yank and a look and she shuts up, and they go on.*)

Jem. Thank you, Mr. Townsend, Sir.

(*They go toward the courthouse.*)

Dill. What's your daddy doin' in the courthouse?

Jem. He's a lawyer and he has a case. The grand jury is charging his client today. I heard somethin' about it when Judge Taylor came over last night.

Dill. Let's go watch.

Jem. Oh, no, Dill . . . He wouldn't like that. No, Dill . . .

(Dill *goes into the courthouse.* Scout *and* Jem *seem worried about following but reluctantly decide to.*)

INTERIOR: COURTHOUSE HALL.

The three children enter. They look around.

Dill. Where's your daddy?

Jem. He'll be in the courtroom. Up there.

(*Moving shot. Dill, Scout, and* Jem *solemnly climb the stairs to the second floor.*)

Dill, wait a minute.

(*There is a small foyer here and a door leading into the courtroom. They go up to the courtroom door.*)

Dill. Is that the courtroom?

Jem. Yeah. Ssh!

Dill (*trying to look into the keyhole*). I can't see anything.

Jem. Ssh!

Dill. You lift me up so I can see what's going on.

Jem. All right. Make a saddle, Scout.

(Jem *and* Scout *make a packsaddle with their arms and* Dill *climbs up and peers in the glass at the top of the door.*)

Dill. Not much is happening. The judge looks like he's asleep. I see your daddy and a colored man. The colored man looks to me like he's crying. I wonder what he's done to cry about?

(Dill *gets so absorbed in watching that he stops talking.* Scout *and* Jem *begin to feel the strain of holding him up.*)

Scout. What's going on?

Dill. There are a lot of men sitting together on one side and one man is pointing at the colored man and yelling. They're taking the colored man away.

Jem. Where is Atticus?

Dill. I can't see your daddy now, either. I wonder where in the world . . .

Atticus (*coming out of a side door and coming toward them*). Scout. Jem. What in the world are you doing here?

(*They whirl around, dropping the startled* Dill.)

Jem. Hello, Atticus.

Atticus. What are you doing here?

Jem. We came down to find out where Boo Radley was locked up. We wanted to see the bats.

Atticus. I want you all back home right away.

Jem. Yes Sir.

Atticus. Run along, now. I'll see you there for dinner.

(*The three children exit down the steps.*)

(Robert E. Lee Ewell, *a short, bantam cock of a man,* approaches Atticus *and blocks his way.*)

Mr. Ewell.

Ewell. Cap'n, I . . . I'm real sorry they picked you to defend that nigger that raped my Mayella. I don't know why I didn't kill him myself instead of goin' for the sheriff. That would have saved you and the sheriff and the taxpayers a lot of trouble.

Atticus. Excuse me, Mr. Ewell, I'm very busy.

Ewell. Hey, Cap'n, somebody told me just now that they thought you believed Tom Robinson's story agin ours. Do you know what I said? I said you're wrong, man . . . you're clear wrong. Mr. Finch ain't takin' his story agin ours.

(Atticus *eyes him impassively.*)

Well, they was wrong, wasn't they?

Atticus. I've been appointed to defend Tom Robinson and now that he's been charged that's what I intend to do.

Ewell. You're takin' his . . .

Atticus. If you'll excuse me, Mr. Ewell . . .

(Atticus *exits as* Ewell *turns, watching him, astounded.*)

Ewell. What kind of a man are you? You got chillun of your own.

EXTERIOR: FINCH PORCH. NIGHT.

> Scout *and* Jem *are sitting there.* Dill *comes running into the yard and over to them.*

Dill. Hey, Jem . . . Jem.

(Jem *goes running toward him.* Scout *follows. The two boys run toward Miss Stephanie's yard.* Scout, Dill, *and* Jem *leap over the wall separating Miss Stephanie's and Atticus' yards.*)

Scout (*cautiously*). I think we ought to stay right here in Miss Stephanie's yard.

Jem. You don't have to come along, Angel May.

(*The boys start to go out of Miss Stephanie's yard.* Scout *follows.*)

(*Moving shot. They walk down the sidewalk silently. They can hear the porch swings creaking with the weight of the neighborhood and the night murmurs of the grown people on the street. They come to the sidewalk in front of the Radley house, and* Jem *looks at the house.* Dill *and* Scout *stand beside him, looking too.*)

Scout. What are you going to do?

Jem. We're going to look in the window of the Radley house and see if we can get a look at Boo Radley. Come on, Dill.

Scout. Jem, please, I'm scared.

Jem (*angrily*). Then go home if you're scared. I swear, Scout, you act more like a girl all the time. Dill, come on.

(Jem *and* Dill *start on.* Scout *watches for a moment, then runs after them.*)

Scout. Wait for me. I'm coming.

Jem (*whispering*). Ssh! We'll go around the back and crawl under the high wire fence at the rear of the Radley lot. I don't believe we can be seen from there.

(*The children go on quietly to the back of the Radley property.*)

Come on!

EXTERIOR: THE BACK OF THE RADLEY PROPERTY.

> *The fence encloses a large garden.* Jem, Scout, *and* Dill *come in.* Jem *holds the bottom wire up and motions* Dill *to crawl under. He does so.* Scout *follows. Then* Scout *holds up the wire for* Jem. *It is a very tight squeeze for him, but he manages to make it.*

Jem (*whispering*). Come on. Now help me. Don't make a sound.

(*The children cautiously approach the house.* Scout *is so intimidated by* Jem's *warning that she moves barely a step a minute; then, when she looks up and sees* Jem *quite a distance ahead, she begins to move faster. They reach the gate which divides the garden from the backyard.* Jem *touches it. The gate squeaks.*)

Dill (*whispering*). Spit on it!

(*The three spit on the gate hinges until they have no spit left.*)

Jem. All right.

(*The gate squeaks again.*)

Scout. Jem.

Jem. Ssh! Spit some more.

(*They try to muster up more spit, and then* Jem *opens the gate slowly, lifting it aside and resting it on the fence.*)

All right.

(*The backyard is even less inviting than the front. A ramshackle porch runs the width of the house. There are two doors and two dark windows between the doors. Instead of a column, a rough two-by-four supports one end of the porch. Above it a hat rack catches the moon and shines eerily.*)

Come on.

(*They cross the yard and go to the back porch.* Jem *puts his foot on the bottom step; the step squeaks. He stands still, then tries his weight by degrees. The step is silent.* Jem *skips two steps, puts his foot on the porch, heaves himself to it, and teeters a long moment. He regains his balance and drops onto his knees. He crawls to a window, raises his head, and looks in.* Scout *suddenly looks up and sees a shadow. It is the shadow of a man. The back porch is bathed in moonlight, and the shadow moves across the porch toward* Jem. Dill *sees it next. He puts his hands to his face. The shadow crosses* Jem. Jem *sees it. He puts his arms over his head and goes rigid. The shadow stops about a foot beyond* Jem. *Its arms come out from its sides, drop, and are still. Then it turns and moves back across* Jem, *walks along the porch and off the side of the house, returning as it had come.* Jem *leaps off the porch and gallops toward* Scout *and* Dill. *He pushes* Dill *and* Scout *through the gate and the collards.*)

Move, move!

(Jem *holds the bottom wire of the fence, and* Scout *and* Dill *roll through.* Jem *starts under the fence and is caught. He struggles as the wire holds his pants.* Jem *looks up, terrified, as he tries to pull free.*)

Scout!

(Scout *and* Dill *run to him.*)

Scout!

(Jem *is on his hands and knees under the fence.* Scout *kneels down and tries to free* Jem's *pants.* Scout *and* Dill *remove* Jem's *pants as he kicks and struggles. Then he rises.*)

(*Moving shot. They run.*)

Scout. Quick—over here.

(Jem, Scout, *and* Dill *continue running through the bushes behind their garage. They are frightened and breathing hard. They all fall to their knees and huddle against the garage wall. They look at one another but are unable to speak.* Dill *cannot get his breath and starts to cough.*)

Ssh! Ssh!

(Dill *buries his head in his knees.* Jem *finally gets up and peers around the corner of the garage.* Scout *watches him.*)

Scout (*whispering*). What are you going to do for pants, Jem?

Jem. I don't know.

Stephanie (*calling off camera*). Dill! Dill! You come on in now.

(*They all jump.* Dill *turns to the others, very frightened.*)

Dill. I'd better go.

Stephanie (*shouting off camera*). Dill!

Dill (*calling*). Coming, Aunt Stephanie. (*Whispering to* Jem *and* Scout.) So long. I'll see you next summer.

Jem. So long.

Scout. So long.

(Dill *runs across the driveway and climbs the fence into Miss Stephanie's yard.*)

Stephanie (*calling*). Dill!

Dill. I'm coming.

Jem. I'm going back after my pants.

Scout. Oh, please, Jem, come on in the house.

Jem. I can't go in without my pants. (*He starts to go.*)

Scout. Well, I'm going to call Atticus.

Jem (*grabbing her collar and wrenching it tight*). No, you're not. Now listen. Atticus ain't never whipped me since I can remember, and I plan to keep it that way.

Scout. Then I'm going with you.

Jem. No, you ain't. You stay right here. I'll be back before you can count to ten.

(Scout *watches* Jem *vault over the low fence and disappear in the high bushes. She starts counting.*)

Scout. One . . . two . . . three . . . four . . .

Atticus (*calling*). Jem. Scout. Come on in.

Scout (*counting*). . . . five . . . six . . . seven . . . eight . . . nine . . . ten . . . eleven . . . twelve . . . thirteen . . . fourteen . . .

(*There is a sound of a shotgun blast.* Scout *stands there stunned. Suddenly she shuts her eyes and presses her hands* over her ears. *She looks as if she's about to scream. At that moment,* Jem *bursts through the bushes and jumps the fence, crashing into* Scout.)

Jem!

Jem (*clapping his hand over her mouth*). Ssh! (*He begins frantically to pull on his pants.*)

(*There is the sound of dogs barking.*)

EXTERIOR: STREET IN FRONT OF THE RADLEY HOUSE.

> Atticus *and* Miss Maudie *are there talking to* Mr. Radley, *who is holding a shotgun. They both start up the street toward Miss Stephanie's house.* Miss Stephanie *comes running off her front porch, pulling on a robe over her nightgown.*

Stephanie. What's going on? What happened? What's going on? What is it? Atticus, what is it? Will somebody please tell me what's going on?

Atticus. Mr. Radley shot at a prowler out in his collard patch.

Stephanie. A prowler. Oh, Maudie . . . (*Moves to* Maudie, *who comforts her.*)

Maudie. Well, whoever it was won't be back any time soon. Mr. Radley must have scared them out of their wits.

Atticus. Well, good night.

Stephanie. Good night.

Maudie. Good night, Atticus.

(Atticus *goes toward his house, and* Maudie *and* Stephanie *go toward Stephanie's house.*)

Stephanie. Oh, it scared the living daylights out of me.

(Atticus *sees* Scout *and* Jem *in the yard.*)

Atticus. Come on in the house. The excitement is over. Time for bed. Scout. Jem.

(Scout *and* Jem *look at each other. Then they start for the house. As they climb the steps,* Jem *looks back over his shoulder toward the Radley house.*)

INTERIOR: FINCH KITCHEN. THE NEXT MORNING.

> Atticus *and* Jem *are eating breakfast.* Calpurnia *is serving them.* Miss Maudie *comes into the kitchen.*

Maudie. Good morning.

Calpurnia. Good morning, Miss Maudie.

Atticus. Good morning, Maudie.

Calpurnia (*going to the hall door and calling*). Scout!

Maudie. I came to see Jean Louise ready for her first day of school.

(Calpurnia *gets the coffeepot from the stove.*)

Hey, Jem.

Calpurnia (*calling*). Scout! (*Pours the coffee.*)

Atticus. What are you going to do with yourself all morning, Cal, with both the children in school?

Calpurnia. I don't know, and that's the truth. I was thinking about that just now. (*Goes back to the hall door and calls.*) Scout! Scout! Did you hear me, Scout? Now hurry!

(Calpurnia *comes back in, and* Scout *follows. She has on a dress and feels very awkward in it.* Jem *sees her.*)

Jem. Hey, everybody . . . look at Scout!

(*He is about to make a comment and laugh, but* Miss Maudie *gives him a poke.*)

Maudie. Ssh!

Atticus. Come on in, Scout.

(Jem *giggles.*)

Have your breakfast.

Maudie. I think your dress is mighty becoming, honey.

(Scout *is not reassured; she begins to tug at it.* Miss Maudie *nods her head to* Atticus *to let him know she approves of the dress.*)

Calpurnia. Now, don't go tugging at that dress, Scout. You want to have it all wrinkled before you even get to school?

Scout. I still don't see why I have to wear a darn old dress.

Maudie. You'll get used to it.

(Scout *sits at the table and starts to eat.* Jem *has eaten his breakfast—all he's going to—and gets up.*)

Jem. I'm ready.

Atticus. Jem! It's half an hour before school starts. Sit right down and wait for your sister.

Jem (*returning to the table and sitting*). Well, hurry up, Scout.

Scout. I'm trying to. (*Takes a few halfhearted bites, then gets up.*)

Jem. Well, come on . . . it's your first day. Do you want to be late?

Scout. I'm ready.

Jem. Come on, let's go.

(Jem *exits as* Scout *drops her books in the doorway. She picks them up and then runs to* Atticus *and kisses his cheek. She runs out the door as* Jem *runs in, grabbing his books.*)

Scout. Bye.

Jem. Goodbye, everyone!

(Miss Maudie, Atticus, *and* Calpurnia *go as far as the screen door with them.* Scout *and* Jem *go out of the screen door.*)

EXTERIOR: SCHOOL GROUNDS

> Scout *sees* Walter Cunningham, Jr., *seven, standing in the school yard. She grabs him, throws him down, and begins to rub his nose in the dirt.*

Scout. Darn you, Walter Cunningham.

(*The other children gather around, watching the fight.* Walter *and* Scout *are on the ground. She pounds him on the back with her fists.* Jem *comes running up and pulls her off.*)

Jem. Cut that out! What do you think you're doing?

Scout. He made me start off on the wrong foot. I was trying to explain to that darn lady teacher why he didn't have no money for his lunch, and she got sore at me.

Jem (*continuing to hold her as they struggle*). Stop it! Stop it!

(*A group of children have gathered around* Jem *holding* Scout. *He releases her.* Jem *walks to* Walter *as the others start to disperse.* Walter *has picked himself up and stands with his fists half-cocked.* Jem *looks him over.*)

Your daddy Mr. Walter Cunningham from Old Sarum?

(Walter *nods his head "yes."*)

Well, come home and have dinner with us, Walter. We'd be glad to have you.

(Walter's *face brightens, then darkens.*)

Well, our daddy's a friend of your daddy's. Scout here is crazy. She won't fight you no more.

(Walter *stands biting his lip, thinking but not answering.*)

INTERIOR: FINCH LIVING ROOM—DINING ROOM.

> *The living room is comfortable but unpretentiously furnished. There are a sofa, two overstuffed chairs, and a rocker in the room. Through an alcove the dining room can be seen. The table is set for dinner and* Jem, Scout, *and* Walter *are there with* Atticus. Calpurnia *is serving the food.*

Atticus. That's a dinner that you'll enjoy.

(Walter *looks down at his plate. There are string beans, roast, corn bread, turnips, and rice.* Walter *looks at* Atticus.)

Walter. Yes Sir. I don't know when I've had a roast. We've been having squirrels and rabbits lately. My pa and I go hunting in our spare time.

Jem. You got a gun of your own?

Walter. Uh huh.

Jem. How long have you had a gun?

Walter. Oh, a year or so.

(Jem *looks at* Atticus.)

Can I have the syrup, please?

Atticus. Certainly, Son. (*Calls to* Calpurnia.) Cal, will you please bring in the syrup dish?

Calpurnia (*calling back*). Yes Sir.

Jem. How old were you when you got your first gun, Atticus?

Atticus. Thirteen or fourteen. I remember when my daddy gave me that gun. He told me that I should never point it at anything in the house. And that he'd rather I'd just shoot tin cans in the backyard, but he said that sooner or later he supposed the temptation to go after birds would be too much, and that I could shoot all the blue jays I wanted, if I could hit them, but to remember it is a sin to kill a mockingbird.

Jem. Why?

Atticus. Well, I reckon because mockingbirds don't do anything but make music for us to enjoy. They don't eat people's gardens, don't nest in the corncribs, they don't do one thing but just sing their hearts out for us. (*Looks at* Scout.) How did you like school, Scout?

Scout. All right.

(Calpurnia *enters with the syrup dish.*)

Atticus. Oh, thank you, Cal. That's for Walter.

(*She takes the dish to* Walter. *He begins to pour it liberally all over his food.* Scout *is watching this process. She makes a face of disgust.*)

Scout. What in the Sam Hill are you doing, Walter?

(Atticus's *hand thumps the table beside her.*)

But, Atticus . . . he has gone and drowned his dinner in syrup.

(*The silver saucer clatters.* Walter *places the pitcher on it and quickly puts his hands in his lap and ducks his head.* Atticus *shakes his head at* Scout *to keep quiet.*)

Calpurnia. Scout!

Scout. What?

Calpurnia. Come out here. I want to talk to you.

(Scout *eyes her suspiciously, sees she is in no mood to be trifled with, and goes out to the kitchen.* Calpurnia *stalks after her.*)

INTERIOR: KITCHEN.

      Scout *and* Calpurnia *enter.*

Calpurnia. That boy is your company. And if he wants to eat up that tablecloth, you let him, you hear? And if you can't act fit to eat like folks, you can just set here and eat in the kitchen. (*Sends her back into the dining room with a smack.*)

INTERIOR: LIVING ROOM—DINING ROOM.

      Atticus, Jem, *and* Walter *continue eating as* Scout *runs through the dining room and living room to the front porch.*

EXTERIOR: FRONT PORCH.

      Scout *sits on the swing.*

Atticus (*calling*). Scout! (*Comes out on the porch.*) Scout. Scout, what in the world's got into you? Now, now . . . (*Sits on the swing next to her.*)

Scout. Atticus, I'm not going back to school anymore.

Atticus. Now, Scout, it's just the first day.

Scout. I don't care. Everything went wrong. My teacher got mad as the devil at me and said you were teaching me to read all wrong and to stop it. And then she acted like a fool and tried to give Walter Cunningham a quarter when everybody knows Cunninghams won't take nothin' from nobody. Any fool could have told her that.

Atticus. Well, maybe she's just nervous. After all, it's her first day, too, teachin' school and bein' new here.

Scout. Oh, Atticus.

Atticus. Now, wait a minute. If you can learn a single trick, Scout, you'll get along a lot better with all kinds of folks. You never really understand a person until you consider things from his point of view.

Scout. Sir?

Atticus. Until you climb inside of his skin and walk around in it.

Scout. But if I keep goin' to school, we can't ever read anymore.

Atticus. Scout, do you know what a compromise is?

Scout. Bending the law?

Atticus. No. It's an agreement reached by mutual consent. Now, here's the way it works. You concede the necessity of goin' to school, we'll keep right on readin' every night, the same as we always have. Is that a bargain?

(Scout *and* Atticus *continue talking as* Jean Louise's *voice is heard.*)

Jean Louise (*voice over*). There just didn't seem to be anyone or thing Atticus couldn't explain. Though it wasn't a talent that would arouse the admiration of any of our friends. Jem and I had to admit he was very good at that, but that was all he was good at, we thought.

EXTERIOR: FINCH HOUSE. DAY.

> Scout *and* Jem *are playing, using sticks as guns.* Scout *stops and watches* Jem *for a beat.*

Scout. What are you looking at?

Jem. That old dog down yonder.

Scout. That's old Tim Johnson, ain't it? What's he doing?

Jem. I don't know, Scout. We better get inside.

(*They run into the house.*)

EXTERIOR: FRONT PORCH OF FINCH HOUSE. DAY.

> Scout, Jem, *and* Calpurnia *come out of the house onto the front porch and look down the road.*

Jem. See, there he is.

(*They see the dog, not much more than a speck in the distance, walking erratically as if his right legs were shorter than his left legs. He snarls and jumps.* Calpurnia *turns to* Jem *and* Scout *and makes them go inside.*)

Calpurnia. Scout, Jem, come on inside. Come on, come on, get in!

INTERIOR: KITCHEN. DAY.

> Calpurnia *and the children run into the kitchen. She goes to the telephone, shouting in her excitement.*

Calpurnia. Mr. Finch? This is Cal. I swear to God there's a mad dog comin' down the street a piece. He's comin' this way.

EXTERIOR: FINCH HOUSE. DAY.

> *It is quiet and deserted. A black Ford swings into the driveway. Atticus and the sheriff, Heck Tate, get out. Tate carries a heavy rifle. Calpurnia comes out on the porch. She points down the street. The children stare out of the screen door. There is a total stillness. Heck Tate sniffs and then blows his nose. He shifts the gun to the crook of his arm.*

Atticus (*softly*). There he is.

(*The dog comes into sight, walking dazedly in the inner rim of a curve parallel to the Radley place.*)

Tate. He's got it all right, Mr. Finch.

(*The dog is still advancing at a snail's pace. He seems dedicated to one course and motivated by an invisible force that inches him toward the Finches'. He reaches the street which runs in front of the Radley place. He pauses as if with what is left of his poor mind he is trying to consider what road to take. He makes a few hesitant steps, reaches the Radley gate, tries to turn around, but is having difficulty.*)

Atticus. He's within range, Heck.

Tate. Take him, Mr. Finch.

(*He hands the rifle to Atticus.*)

Scout (*calling out*). Oh, no, Mr. Tate. He don't shoot.

Atticus. Don't waste time, Heck.

Tate. For God's sake, Mr. Finch, he's got to be killed right away before he starts runnin'. Look where he is. I can't shoot that well. You know it.

Atticus. I haven't shot a gun in twenty years.

Tate (*almost throwing the gun at* Atticus). I'd feel mighty comfortable if you did now.

(Atticus *accepts the gun. He walks out of the yard and to the middle of the street. He raises his glasses, pushes them to his forehead. They slip down, and he drops them in the street. In the silence, we can hear them crack.* Atticus, *blinking hard, rubs his eyes and his chin. The dog has made up his mind. He takes two steps forward, stops, raises his head. The dog's body goes rigid.* Atticus *brings the gun to his shoulder. The rifle cracks. The dog leaps, flops over, and crumples on the sidewalk.* Heck Tate *runs toward the Radleys'.* Atticus *stoops, picks up his glasses and grinds the broken lens to powder, and walks toward the dog.*)

(Jem *and* Scout *are dumbfounded.* Scout *regains her senses first and pinches* Jem *to get him moving. They run out of the door.* Heck Tate *and* Atticus *are walking toward the house. They meet the still awestruck* Scout *and* Jem. *The children approach* Atticus *reverently.*)

Atticus. Don't go near that dog, you understand? He's just as dangerous dead as alive.

Jem. Yes Sir, Atticus. Atticus?

Atticus. Yes, Son.

Jem. Nothin'.

Tate. What's the matter, boy? Can't you talk? Didn't you know your daddy's the best shot in this county?

Atticus. Oh, hush, Heck. Let's get back to town. Remember now, don't go near that dog.

Jem. Yes Sir.

Tate. I'll send Zeebo out right away to pick him up.

(*He and* Atticus *get into the car and drive off.* Jem *and* Scout, *still stunned, watch them go.*)

EXTERIOR: FINCH GARAGE. NIGHT.

> Atticus *backs the car out. It is an old car,*
> *not very well kept.* Scout *and* Jem *come*
> *running toward him.*

Jem. Atticus, can we go with you, please?

Scout. Can we?

(Atticus *keeps the motor running and calls out of the window.*)

Atticus. No, I have to go to the country on business, and you'll just get tired.

Scout. No. Not me, I won't get tired.

Atticus. Well, will you promise to stay in the car while I go in and talk to Helen Robinson?

Scout. Uh huh.

Atticus. And not nag about leavin' if you do get tired?

Jem. No.

Atticus. All right. Climb in.

(Scout *and* Jem *run for the car.* Jem *gets in the backseat,* Scout *gets in beside her father.*)

Scout. Who's Helen Robinson?

Atticus. The wife of the man I'm defending.

(*The car moves on.* Scout *is asleep in the front seat in a few minutes.* Atticus *looks down and sees she is and pulls her closer to him.*)

EXTERIOR: TOM ROBINSON'S HOUSE AND YARD. NIGHT.

> *It is a small, neat house and yard. Tom's son, Jem's age, is playing in the yard. Atticus' car drives up. The boy stops playing and watches the car.* Helen Robinson, *twenty-nine, comes to the door of the house. She has a baby in her arms, and three small children hang on her dress.* Atticus *gets out of the car and goes to the porch. He calls to the boy.*

Atticus. Evening, David.

David. Evening.

Atticus. Evening, Helen.

Helen. Evening, Mr. Finch.

Atticus. I came over to tell you about my visit with Tom.

Helen. Yes.

Atticus. And to let you know that I got a postponement.

(Helen *holds the door open for* Atticus, *and they go in. The boy,* David, *stares at* Jem *for a beat. They wave at each other. He then looks off toward the dirt road.* Jem *turns and looks in the same direction. Down the dirt road, drunk, toward the car, comes* Bob Ewell. Jem *is frightened and starts to leave the car, and then remembers the sleeping* Scout. *He climbs into the front seat beside his sister, all the while watching the approach of* Ewell.)

Jem (*calling to* David). Tell my daddy to come out here, please.

(David *runs into the house.*)

(Jem *gets close to* Scout *and watches* Ewell *get closer and closer.* Ewell *comes right up to the car and stares in the window at* Scout *and* Jem. *He is unshaven and looks as if he'd been on a long drunk. He is unsteady and holds on to the side of the car, staring at the two children.* Atticus *comes to the car.* Ewell *stares drunkenly at him.* Atticus *gets in the car beside* Scout.)

Atticus. No need to be afraid of him, Son. He's all bluff.

(Ewell *takes a swig of whiskey from a bottle he has taken from his back pocket and goes reeling off down the road.* Jem *climbs in the back seat.* Atticus *starts the car.* Atticus *turns the car around and goes slowly back down the dirt road. The lights of the car pick up* Ewell *standing drunkenly in the middle of the road looking like some terrible figure of wrath.* Atticus *has to slow the car down to almost a crawl in order to pass* Ewell *without hitting him. As he passes,* Ewell *yells.*)

Ewell. Nigger lover!

(Jem *leans across the front seat and puts his hand on his father's shoulder.* Atticus *senses the boy's fright and pats his hand.* Scout *sleeps through it all. They drive on, leaving the drunken fury of a man shouting in the darkness.*)

EXTERIOR: FINCH HOUSE. NIGHT.

> Atticus *drives the car up. He glances back at* Jem.

Atticus. There's a lot of ugly things in this world, Son. I wish I could keep 'em all away from you. That's never possible.

(Atticus *leans down and lifts the sleeping* Scout *off the seat. He carries* Scout *toward the house as* Calpurnia *comes out from the kitchen.*)

If you wait until I get Scout in bed, I'll drive you home.

Calpurnia. Yes Sir.

(Atticus *starts for the house. Jem* sits on the porch in the *rocking chair.*)

Atticus (*coming out*). Jem, would you mind staying here with Scout until I get Cal home?

Jem. No Sir.

Calpurnia. Night, Jem.

Jem. Night, Cal.

(Jem *sees his father and* Calpurnia *get into the car and start off. A tree rustles, a shadow passes over the porch where* Jem *sits, a night bird calls. He is struck with sudden terror.*)

(*Moving shot. He starts to run toward the Radley place in the direction of his father's car.* Jem *runs awhile longer, past the Radley oak, calling "Atticus, Atticus." He realizes it is futile and stops. He freezes. He sees something gleaming and reflecting the moonlight in the knothole of the oak tree, where it is hollow. He stops, looks around, sticks his hand in the knothole, and takes out a shiny medal. He quickly puts it in his pocket. He runs past the Radley house, into his yard, and into the house.*)

EXTERIOR: SCHOOL GROUNDS. DAY.

> Scout *and two other girls are jumping rope. A boy,* Cecil Jacobs, *who is* Scout's *age, pulls the rope away, ending the jumping. He and* Scout *face each other in anger. Other kids group around as they argue.* Scout *jumps on* Cecil *and throws him to the ground as they fight. The other children gather around and begin yelling, egging them on.* Jem *rushes in and pulls* Scout *off* Cecil, *as she struggles.* Cecil *runs off. The other children move away.*

Jean Louise (*voice over*). Atticus had promised me he would wear me out if he ever heard of me fightin' any more. I was far too old and too big for such childish things, and the sooner I learned to hold in, the better off everybody would be. I soon forgot . . . Cecil Jacobs made me forget.

EXTERIOR: FINCH FRONT PORCH. AFTERNOON.

> Scout *sits on the front steps, her head buried in her arms.* Atticus *comes into the yard.* Scout *looks up.*

Atticus. Well, what is it, Scout?

Scout. Atticus, do you defend niggers?

Atticus. Don't say "nigger," Scout.

Scout. I didn't say it . . . Cecil Jacobs did. That's why I had to fight him.

Atticus (*sternly*). Scout, I don't want you fightin'!

Scout. I had to, Atticus . . . He . . .

Atticus (*interrupting*). I don't care what the reasons are. I forbid you to fight.

Scout. Yes Sir.

(Atticus *sits down beside* Scout, *putting his hat and briefcase down on the porch.*)

Atticus. Anyway, I'm simply defending a Negro, Tom Robinson. Scout . . . there are some things you're not old enough to understand just yet. There's been some high talk around town to the effect that I shouldn't do much about defending this man.

Scout (*looking up*). If you shouldn't be defending him, then why are you doing it?

Atticus (*putting his arm around* Scout, *hugging her close to him*). For a number of reasons. The main one is if I didn't, I couldn't hold my head up in this town. I couldn't even tell you and Jem not to do somethin' again. Scout, you're gonna hear some ugly talk about this in school. But I want you to promise me one thing . . . that you won't get into fights over it, no matter what they say to you.

Scout (*breaking loose*). Yes Sir.

(Atticus *gets up and goes inside the house.* Scout *sees* Jem *on the sidewalk and goes toward him. He is walking most peculiarly, with his feet out and his arms held to his sides. He is doing an imitation of ancient Egyptians.* Scout *runs to meet him. When she gets five feet from him, she becomes aware of his peculiar walk and stops and looks more closely.*)

What are you doing?

Jem. Walking like an Egyptian. We were studyin' about them in school. Teacher says we wouldn't be no place without them.

Scout. Is that so?

(*She begins to try to imitate his walk. They go toward the Radleys'.*)

Jem. Cradle of civilization. They invented embalming and toilet paper . . . (*He sees her imitation. He stops and goes to her, kneels and takes her feet.*) That's wrong, Scout. You do your feet this way. (*He takes her feet and tries to fix them. He is kneeling in front of the Radley oak tree with the knothole. While he is kneeling,* Scout *glances around at the oak and sees two figures carved out of soap in the knothole.*)

Scout. Look, Jem.

(*She points to the figures and gets close beside him and peers at them. He tenderly takes the two soap figures out of the knothole. One is the figure of a boy. The other wears a crude dress.*)

Look . . . the boy has hair in front of his eyebrows like you do.

Jem. And the girl wears bangs like you . . . these are us!

(Mr. Radley *enters from behind the tree and looks at* Jem. Jem *jumps back, frightened.* Mr. Radley *starts filling the knothole with cement from a trowel.* Jem *and* Scout *stand watching him. They start to back away, and then go running down the street, as* Mr. Radley *continues filling the hole with cement.*)

INTERIOR: JEM'S ROOM. NIGHT.

> Jem *is seated on the bed with an open cigar box in front of him. He picks up both dolls and puts them inside the box and closes it quickly as* Scout *enters the room.*

Scout. Jem . . . are you awake?

Jem. Go back to bed!

(*She moves to the bed and sits down at the foot of it.*)

Scout. I can't go to sleep.

Jem. Go back to bed!

(*She notices the cigar box.*)

Scout. What you got in the box?

Jem. Nothin'. Go back to bed!

Scout. Come on.

Jem. If I show you, will you swear never to tell anybody?

Scout. I swear . . .

Jem. Cross your heart . . .

(*She crosses her heart with her left hand and raises it in a swearing gesture, then lowers it and waits as* Jem *takes the box and opens the top. They look in the box. There is a spelling medal, a pocket watch, some pennies, a broken pocketknife. He takes the medal out and holds it up for* Scout *to see. She is wide-eyed.*)

I found all these in the knothole of that ole tree . . . at different times. This is a spelling medal. You know, they used to award these in school to spelling winners before we were born. And another time I found this . . . (*He picks up the pocket watch.*) And this . . . (*He holds up the pocketknife.*) And Scout, you know something else I never told you about that night I went back to the Radleys'?

Scout. Something else? You never told me anything about that night.

Jem. Well . . . you know the first time when I was gittin' outta my britches?

Scout. Uh huh.

Jem. Well, they was all in a tangle, and I couldn't get 'em loose. Well, when I went back, though, they were folded across the fence . . . sorta like they was expectin' me.

(Scout *is looking at the watch. She is goggle-eyed.* Jem *holds the soap figures of the boy and the girl he found in the knothole.*)

Jean Louise (*voice over*). It was to be a long time before Jem and I talked about Boo again.

INTERIOR: FINCH KITCHEN. DAY.

> Calpurnia *is at the sink.* Scout *and* Jem *are eating.* Dill *comes in.*

Jean Louise (*voice over*). School finally ended and summer came . . . and so did Dill.

Dill. Good mornin'.

Calpurnia. Good mornin'. My, you're up mighty bright and early.

Dill. Oh, I've been up since four.

Calpurnia. Four?

Dill. Oh, yes, I always get up at four. It's in my blood. You see, my daddy was a railroad man till he got rich. Now he flies airplanes. One of these days, he's just goin' to swoop down here to Maycomb, pick me up, and take me for a ride.

EXTERIOR: FINCH HOUSE. LATE AFTERNOON.

> Atticus *sits on the porch reading as* Jem *comes out with a pitcher of juice. He moves back to* Atticus *and puts the pitcher on the chair beside him, then he takes a cookie from a plate on the chair.* Atticus *lifts his briefcase and starts putting his papers inside. The Sheriff's car comes by.*

Jem. Who's that in the car with Sheriff Tate?

Atticus (*looking up*). Tom Robinson, Son.

Jem. Where's he been?

Atticus. In the Abbottsville jail.

Jem. Why?

Atticus. The sheriff thought he'd be safer there.

They're bringin' him back here tonight because his trial is tomorrow. (*He gets up and goes into the house.*)

INTERIOR: JEM'S ROOM. NIGHT.

> *In his room,* Jem *is lying in bed beside the sleeping* Dill. *He hears a knock at the screen door.*

INTERIOR: LIVING ROOM. NIGHT.

> Atticus *goes to the door and opens it.* Heck Tate *is standing there.*

Atticus. Well, good evenin', Heck.

Tate. Evenin', Mr. Finch.

Atticus. Come in.

Tate (*coming in*). The news has gotten 'round the county about my bringin' Tom Robinson back to the jail. I heard there might be trouble from that bunch out at Old Sarum.

INTERIOR: KITCHEN. NIGHT.

> Atticus *goes into the kitchen to* Calpurnia.

Atticus. Cal, if I need you to stay here tonight, can you do it?

Calpurnia. Yes Sir . . . I can.

Atticus. Thank you. I think you better count on stayin'.

Calpurnia. Yes Sir.

(Atticus *goes out.* Calpurnia *goes back to work.*)

INTERIOR: JEM'S ROOM. NIGHT.

> Jem *is lying in bed, still awake.* Dill *is asleep.* Atticus *comes in and gets something from the shelf and goes out again.* Jem *gets out of bed and listens by the door. He gets his clothes from the closet and starts to get dressed.* Dill *awakens and sits up in bed.* Scout *comes into the room.*

Dill. What's going on?

Jem. Sssh. Go back to sleep!

Scout. What's going on?

Jem. Sssshhh!

(The three of them go out of the room.)

EXTERIOR: FINCH HOUSE. NIGHT.

> *They come outside and walk down the sidewalk toward town.*

EXTERIOR: TOWN SQUARE. NIGHT.

> *It is deserted and dark. The stores around the square are dark except for night lights burning back by the safes and cash registers.*

> *Moving shot. The three children walk down the street by Atticus' office. They see his car parked in front of the building. They look in the doorway of the building. It is dark.* Jem *tries the knob of the door. It is locked.*

Jem. Hey, there's his car.

(They walk up the sidewalk. They see a solitary light burning in the distance. It is from the jail. As they approach the jail,

they can see the long extension cord Atticus *brought from the house running between the bars of the second-floor window and down the side of the building. In the light from its bare bulb they see* Atticus *propped against the front door. He is sitting on one of the office chairs, and he is reading a newspaper, oblivious of the night bugs hovering above his head.)*

See, there he is . . . over there!

(Scout starts to run toward him.)

No, Scout . . . don't go to him. He might not like it. I just wanted to see where he was and what he was up to. He's all right. Let's go back home. Come on.

(The children start back across the square, taking a shortcut, when they hear a noise and pause. They see four dusty cars come in from the Meridian Highway, moving slowly, in a line. They go around the square, pass the bank building, and stop in front of the jail. Nobody gets out. Atticus *looks up from his newspaper, closes it, deliberately folds it, drops it in his lap, and pushes his hat to the back of his head. He seems to be expecting the men.* Scout, Jem, *and* Dill *run to the cover of some bushes and hide behind them, watching.)*

(In ones and twos, the men get out of the cars. They are country men. Walter Cunningham, Sr., *is among them. They surround* Atticus.*)*

Man. He in there, Mr. Finch?

Atticus. He is. He's asleep. Don't wake him.

Cunningham. You know what we want. Get aside from that door, Mr. Finch.

Atticus. Walter, I think you ought to turn right around and go back home. Heck Tate's around here somewhere.

Kelley. No, he ain't. Heck's bunch is out chasin' around Ole Sarum lookin' for us.

Tex. We knowed he was, so we came around the other way.

Kelley. And you hadn't never thought about that, had you, Mr. Finch?

Atticus. I thought about it.

(*The children run over to the car.*)

Scout. I can't see Atticus.

(Scout *darts out toward the men,* Dill *behind her, before* Jem *can reach out and grab them.*)

Atticus. Well, that changes things, doesn't it?

(Scout *and* Dill *run,* Jem *behind them. They run to the men and push themselves through until they reach* Atticus.)

Scout. Atticus!

(*She smiles up at him, but when she catches the look of fear on his face, she becomes insecure.* Scout *looks around at the men surrounding her. Most are strangers to her.*)

Hey, Atticus . . .

(Atticus *gets up from his chair and begins to move slowly, like an old man, toward them.*)

Atticus. Jem, go home. And take Scout and Dill home with you.

(Scout *looks up at* Jem. *She sees he is not thinking of leaving.* Jem *shakes his head "no."* Atticus' *fists go to his hips and so do* Jem's, *and they face each other in defiance.*)

Son, I said, "Go home!"

Jem. No Sir!

(Jem *shakes his head. A burly man grabs* Jem *roughly by the collar.*)

Man. I'll send him home!

(*The man almost yanks* Jem *off his feet.* Atticus *flushes. His fists clench; he reaches for* Jem. *But before he gets to him,* Scout *kicks the man swiftly.*)

Scout. Don't you touch him! Let 'im go! Let 'im go!

(*The man falls back in pain.* Atticus *puts his hand on her shoulder.*)

Atticus. That'll do, Scout.

Scout. Ain't nobody gonna do Jem that-a-way.

Man (*growling in the back*). Now, you get 'em outta here, Mr. Finch.

Atticus. Jem, I want you to please leave.

Jem. No Sir.

Atticus. Jem!

Jem. I tell ya, I ain't goin'!

(Scout *becomes bored by this exchange; she looks back at the men. She sees a man she recognizes. She moves toward him.*)

Scout. Hey, Mr. Cunningham . . .

(Walter Cunningham, Sr., *does not seem to hear her.*)

I said, "Hey," Mr. Cunningham. How's your entailment getting along?

(*The man blinks and hooks his thumbs into his overall straps. He seems uncomfortable. He clears his throat and looks away.* Scout *walks a little closer to him.*)

Don't you remember me, Mr. Cunningham? I'm Jean Louise Finch. You brought us some hickory nuts early one morning, remember? We had a talk. I went and got my daddy to come out and thank you. I go to school with your boy. I go to school with Walter. He's a nice boy. Tell him "hey" for me, won't you? You know something, Mr. Cunningham, entailments are bad. Entailments . . .

(*Suddenly,* Scout *realizes she is the center of everyone's attention: the men, her brother,* Dill, Atticus. *She becomes self-conscious. She turns to* Atticus.)

Atticus, I was just sayin' to Mr. Cunningham that entailments were bad but not to worry. Takes a long time sometimes . . .

(*She begins to dry up. She looks up at the country men staring at her. They are quite still.*)

What's the matter?

(*She looks at* Atticus. *He says nothing. She looks back at* Mr. Cunningham.)

I sure meant no harm, Mr. Cunningham.

Cunningham. No harm taken, young lady. (*He moves forward and takes* Scout *by the shoulders.*) I'll tell Walter you said "hey," little lady. (*He straightens up and waves a big hand.*) Let's clear outta here. Let's go, boys.

(*As they had come, in ones and twos, the men straggle back into their cars. We hear doors slam, engines cough, and the cars drive off.* Scout, Jem, *and* Dill *watch them leave.*)

Atticus. Now you go home, all of you. I'll be there later.

Jem. Come on . . . come on.

(*The three children go on down the street.* Atticus *sits again in the chair, waiting.* Tom Robinson *calls out from the darkness of the jail.*)

Tom (*off camera*). Mr. Finch . . . they gone?

Atticus. They've gone. They won't bother you any more.

(*He sits back in his chair and continues watching.*)

EXTERIOR: STREET IN FRONT OF FINCH HOUSE. EARLY MORNING. DAY.

> *People are coming from all parts of the county for the trial. It is like Saturday. Wagons carrying country people on the way to the trial stream past the house. Some men ride horseback. Scout, Jem, and Dill sit on the curb of the sidewalk watching the wagons and the horses go by.*

Jem. Morning, Mr. Stevens. How do you do?

(*A man rides by on a mule and waves to the children, and they wave back. A wagonload of ladies rides past. They wear cotton sunbonnets and dresses with long sleeves. A bearded man in a wool hat drives them. A wagonload of stern-faced citizens comes by next.*)

Scout. Did you ever see so many people? Just like on Saturday . . .

(*Jem suddenly gets up.*)

Where you goin'?

Jem. I can't stand it any longer. I'm goin' downtown to the courthouse to watch.

Scout. You better not! You know what Atticus said.

Jem. I don't care if he did. I'm not gonna miss the most excitin' thing that ever happened in this town!

(*They all look at each other and start toward town.*)

EXTERIOR: COURTHOUSE SQUARE. DAY.

> *It is deserted, as everyone is inside watching the trial. Scout, Jem, and Dill come into the square. They stand looking up at the courthouse. They all start toward the entrance. Scout, Jem, and Dill go up the stairs toward the entrance.*

INTERIOR: ENTRANCE HALL OF COURTHOUSE. DAY.

> *When they get to the entrance, Jem peeks through the hole of the door. He looks back at the other two. Reverend Sykes, the black Baptist preacher, comes up the stairs. The children go over to him.*

Jem. It's packed solid. They're standin' all along the back . . . Reverend!

Sykes. Yes?

Jem. Reverend Sykes, are you goin' upstairs?

Sykes. Yes, I am.

(He starts up the stairs and they follow him.)

INTERIOR: COLORED BALCONY OF COURTHOUSE.

> *Reverend Sykes enters the colored balcony with Jem, Dill, and Scout. He leads them among the black people in the gallery. Four blacks in the front row get up and give them their seats when they see them come in.*

Sykes. Brother John, thanks for holding my seat.

(They sit down and peer over the balcony. The colored balcony runs along three walls of the courtroom like a second-story veranda, and from it the children see everything.)

(*The jury sits to the left under long windows. Sunburned, lanky, they are nearly all farmers, but this is only natural. Townfolk rarely sit on juries. They are either struck or excused. The circuit solicitor and another man,* Atticus, *and* Tom Robinson *sit at tables with their backs to the children. Just inside the railing, which divides the spectators from the court, the witnesses sit in cowhide-bottomed chairs.* Judge Taylor *is on the bench, looking like a sleepy old shark.*)

(Jem, Scout, Dill, *and* Reverend Sykes *are listening intently.*)

Bailiff. This court is now in session. Everybody rise.

(*The* Judge *bangs his gavel.*)

INTERIOR: COURTROOM. LATER.

>   *The solicitor* Mr. Gilmer *is questioning the sheriff* Heck Tate.

Tate. On the night of August twenty-first I was just leavin' my office to go home when Bob . . . Mr. Ewell . . . come in, very excited, he was. And he said, get to his house quick as I could . . . that his girl had been raped. I got in my car and went out there as fast as I could. She was pretty well beat up. I asked her if Tom Robinson beat her like that. She said, "Yes, he did." I asked if he'd taken advantage of her and she said, "Yes, he did." That's all there was to it.

Gilmer. Thank you.

(Atticus *is sitting behind his table, his chair skewed to one side, his legs crossed, and one arm is resting on the back of the chair.*)

Judge. Any questions, Atticus?

Atticus. Yes Sir. Did anybody call a doctor, Sheriff?

Tate. No Sir.

Atticus. Why not?

Tate. Well, I didn't think it was necessary. She was pretty well beat up. Something sho' happened. It was obvious.

Atticus. Now, Sheriff, you say that she was mighty beat up. In what way?

Tate. Well, she was beaten around the head. There were bruises already comin' on her arms. She had a black eye startin' an' . . .

Atticus. Which eye?

Tate. Let's see . . . (*Blinks and runs his hand through his hair. He points to an invisible person five inches in front of him.*) It was her left.

Atticus. Well, now, was that, was her left facing you . . . or lookin' the way that you were?

Tate. Oh, yes . . . that . . . would make it her right eye. It was her right eye, Mr. Finch. Now I remember. She was beaten up on that side of her face.

(Heck Tate *blinks again and then turns and looks at* Tom Robinson *as if something had been made clear to him at the same time.* Tom Robinson *raises his head. Something has been made clear to* Atticus, *too, and he gets to his feet. He walks toward* Heck Tate.)

Atticus. Which side, again, Heck?

Tate. The right side. She had bruises on her arms and she showed me her neck. There were definite finger marks on her gullet.

Atticus. All around her neck? At the back of her throat?

Tate. I'd say they were all around.

(Atticus *nods to* Mr. Gilmer *as he sits down.* Mr. Gilmer *shakes his head at the* Judge. *The* Judge *nods to* Tate, *who rises stiffly and steps down from the witness stand.*)

Judge. Witness may be excused.

Bailiff (*booming out*). Robert E. Lee Ewell . . .

(Bob Ewell *rises and struts to the stand. He raises his right hand, puts his left on the Bible, and is sworn in as a witness.*)

Place your hand on the Bible, please. Do you promise to tell the truth, the whole truth, and nothin' but the truth, so help you God?

Ewell. I do.

Bailiff. Sit down.

(Mr. Gilmer *addresses* Ewell.)

Gilmer. Now, Mr. Ewell . . . will you tell us, just in your own words, what happened on August twenty-first.

Ewell. Well, that night I was comin' in from the woods with a load of kindlin', and I heard Mayella screamin' as I got to the fence. So I dropped my kindlin', and I run into the fence. But when I got loose, I run up to the window and I seen him with my Mayella!

(*The rest of the testimony is drowned out by the people in the courtroom, who begin to murmur with excitement. Judge Taylor begins to bang his desk with his gavel. Heck Tate goes to the aisle, trying to quiet the crowd. Atticus is on his feet, whispering to the Judge. The spectators finally quiet down, and Mr. Gilmer continues.*)

Gilmer. What did you do after you saw the defendant?

Ewell. I ran around the house tryin' to get in, but he done run through the front door just ahead o' me. But I seen who it was, all right. I seen him. And I run in the house and po' Mayella was layin' on the floor squallin'. Then I run for Mr. Tate just as quick as I could.

Gilmer. Uh huh. Thank you, Mr. Ewell.

(Mr. Gilmer *sits down.* Atticus *rises and goes to the stand and faces* Ewell.)

Atticus. Would you mind if I just ask you a few questions, Mr. Ewell?

Ewell. No Sir, Mr. Finch, I sho' wouldn't.

Atticus. Folks were doin' a lot of runnin' that night. Let's see, now, you say that you ran to the window, you ran inside, you ran to Mayella, and you ran to the sheriff. Now, did you, during all the runnin', run for a doctor?

Ewell. There weren't no need to. I seen who done it.

Atticus. Now, Mr. Ewell . . . you've heard the sheriff's testimony. Do you agree with his description of Mayella's injuries?

Ewell. I agree with everything Mr. Tate said. Her eye was blacked. She was mighty beat up . . . mighty.

Atticus. Now, Mr. Ewell, can you . . . er . . . can you read and write?

Ewell. Yes Mr. Finch. I can read and I can write.

Atticus. Good . . . then will you write your name, please. Write there, and show us?

(Atticus *takes paper and pen out of his coat. He hands them to* Ewell. Ewell *looks up and sees* Atticus *and* Judge Taylor *looking at him intently.*)

Ewell. Well, what's so interestin'?

Judge. You're left-handed, Mr. Ewell.

(Ewell *turns angrily to the* Judge.)

Ewell. Well, what's that got to do with it, Judge? I'm a God-fearin' man. That Atticus Finch is tryin' to take advantage of me. You got to watch lawyers like Atticus Finch.

Judge (*banging his gavel*). Quiet! Quiet, Sir! Now the witness may take his seat.

(Ewell *sullenly leaves the witness stand.*)

Bailiff. Mayella Violet Ewell . . .

(*A silence comes over the court as* Mayella Ewell *walks to the witness stand. She is a thick-bodied girl, accustomed to strenuous labor.*)

Put your hand on the Bible, please. Do you swear to tell the truth, the whole truth, and nothing but the truth, so help you God?

(Mayella *nods.* Mr. Gilmer *rises and begins to question her.*)

Gilmer. Now, Mayella, suppose you tell us just what happened, huh?

Mayella (*clearing her throat*). Well, Sir . . . I was sittin' on the porch, and . . . and he comes along. Uh, there's this old chifforobe in the yard . . . and I . . . I said, "You come up here, boy, and bust up this chifforobe, and I'll give you a nickel." So he . . . he come on in the yard and I go into the house to get him the nickel and I turn around, and 'fore I know it, he's on me . . . and I fought and hollered . . . but he had me around the neck, and he hit me again and again, and the next thing I knew, Papa was in the room, a-standin' over me, hollerin', "Who done it, who done it?"

Gilmer. Thank you, Mayella. Your witness, Atticus.

(Gilmer *walks away.* Atticus *gets up smiling. He opens his coat, hooks his thumbs in his vest, walks slowly across the room to the windows.*)

Atticus. Miss Mayella, is your father good to you? I mean, is he easy to get along with?

Mayella. He does tol'able . . .

Atticus. Except when he's drinking?

(*A pause. She glares at* Atticus.)

When he's riled, has he ever beaten you?

(Mayella *looks in* Ewell's *direction.*)

Mayella. My pa's never touched a hair o' my head in my life.

(Atticus' *glasses slip a little and he pushes them back on his head.*)

Atticus. Now, you say that you asked Tom to come in and chop up a . . . what was it?

Mayella. A chifforobe.

Atticus. Was this the first time that you ever asked him to come inside the fence?

Mayella (*acting confused and shrugging*). Yes.

Atticus. Didn't you ever ask him to come inside the fence before?

Mayella (*evasively*). I mighta.

Atticus. But can you remember any other occasion?

Mayella (*shaking her head*). No!

Atticus. You say, "He caught me and he choked me and he took advantage of me," is that right?

(Mayella *nods her head.*)

Do you remember his beating you about the face?

Mayella (*hesitating*). No, I don't recollect if he hit me. I . . . mean . . . yes! He hit me . . . he hit me!

Atticus (*turning*). Thank you! Now, will you identify the man who beat you?

Mayella (*pointing to* Tom). I most certainly will . . . sittin' right yonder.

Atticus. Tom, will you stand up, please? Let's let Mayella have a good look at you.

(Tom Robinson *rises to his feet. It is our first good look at him. He is thirty.* Atticus *goes to the table and picks up a water glass.*)

Tom, will you please catch this?

(Atticus *throws the glass.* Tom *is standing at the defense table. He catches the glass with his right hand.*)

Thank you.

(Atticus *walks to* Tom *and takes the glass.*)

Now then, this time will you please catch it with your left hand?

Tom. I can't, Sir.

Atticus. Why can't you?

Tom. I can't use my left hand at all. I got it caught in a cotton gin when I was twelve years old. All my muscles were torn loose.

(*There are murmurs from the crowd in the courtroom. The* Judge *pounds his gavel.*)

Atticus. Is this the man who raped you?

Mayella. He most certainly is.

Atticus. How?

Mayella. I don't know how. He done . . . it . . . (*She starts to sob.*) He just done it.

Atticus. You have testified that he choked you and he beat you. You didn't say that he sneaked up behind you and knocked you out cold, but that you turned and there he was. Do you want to tell us what really happened?

Mayella. I got somethin' to say. And then I ain't gonna say no more. (*She looks in Tom's direction.*) He took advantage of me.

(Atticus *glances in Mayella's direction with a grim expression. She shouts and gestures with her hands as she speaks.*)

An' if you fine, fancy gentlemen ain't gonna do nothin' about it, then you're just a bunch of lousy, yellow, stinkin' cowards, the . . . the whole bunch of you, and your fancy airs don't come to nothin'. Your Ma'am'in' and your Miss Mayellarin'—it don't come to nothin', Mr. Finch. Not . . . no . . .

(*She bursts into real tears. Her shoulders shake with angry heaving sobs. Atticus has hit her in a way that is not clear to him, but he has had no pleasure in doing it. He sits with his head down. Mayella runs as Ewell and a man grab her.*)

Ewell. You sit down there!

Man. Come on, girl.

(Ewell *holds Mayella's arms and starts for his seat. Ewell helps Mayella to her seat. She hides her head as Ewell sits down.*)

(*The Judge looks in Atticus' direction.*)

Judge. Atticus? Mr. Gilmer?

Gilmer (*rising*). The State rests, Judge.

Bailiff. Tom Robinson, take the stand.

(Tom *stands up and goes to the witness chair.*)

Put your hand on the Bible.

(Tom *puts his hand on the Bible.*)

Do you solemnly swear to tell the truth, the whole truth, and nothing but the truth, so help you God?

Tom. I do.

Bailiff. Sit down!

(*The* Bailiff *turns away as* Tom *starts to sit.* Atticus *starts toward the* Judge *and* Tom.)

Atticus. Tom, were you acquainted with Mayella Violet Ewell?

Tom. Yes Sir. I had to pass her place goin' to and from the field every day.

Atticus. Is there any other way to go?

Tom (*shaking his head*). No Sir. None's I know of.

Atticus. Did she ever speak to you?

Tom. Why, yes Sir. I'd tip m'hat when I'd go by, and one day she ask me to come inside the fence and bust up a chifforobe for her. She give me the hatchet and I broke it up and then she said, "I reckon I'll hafta give you a nickel, won't I?" And I said, "No Ma'am, there ain't no charge." Then I went home. Mr. Finch, that was was last spring, way over a year ago.

Atticus. And did you ever go on the place again?

Tom. Yes Sir.

Atticus. When?

Tom. Well, I went lots of times. Seemed like every time I passed by yonder, she'd have some little somethin' for me to do . . . choppin' kindlin', totin' water for her.

Atticus. What happened to you on the evening of August twenty-first of last year?

Tom. Mr. Finch, I was goin' home as usual that evenin' and I passed the Ewell place. Miss Mayella were on the porch like she said she were.

(The spectators, white and colored, all lean forward. It is very quiet in the room.)

An' she said for me to come there and help her a minute. Well, I went inside the fence and I looked aroun' for some kindlin' to work on, but I didn't see none. An' then she said to come in the house, she . . . she has a door needs fixin' . . . so I follow her inside an' looked at the door an' it looked all right, an' she shut the door. All the time I was wonderin' why it was so quiet like . . . an' it come to me, there was not a child on the place, an' I said to Miss Mayella, where are the chil'ren? An' she said, they all gone to get ice cream. She said it took her a slap year to save seb'm nickels, but she done it, an' they all gone to town.

(Tom runs his hands over his face. He is obviously very uncomfortable.)

Atticus. What did you say then?

Tom. Oh, I . . . I said somethin' like, "Why Miss Mayella, that's right nice o' you to treat 'em." An' she said, "You think so?" Well, I said I best be goin', I couldn't do nothin' for her, an' she said, oh, yes I could. An' I ask her what, and she said to jus' step on the chair yonder an' git that box down from on top of the chifforobe. So I done what she told me, and I was reachin' when the next thing I knew she . . . grabbed me aroun' the legs. She scared me so bad I hopped down an' turned the chair over. That was the only thing, only furniture 'sturbed in that room, Mr. Finch, I swear, when I left it.

Atticus. And what happened after you turned the chair over?

(Tom *comes to a dead stop. He glances at* Atticus, *then at the jury.*)

Tom? You've sworn to tell the whole truth. Will you do it? What happened after that?

Tom (*running his hand nervously over his mouth*). Mr. Finch, I got down off the chair, and I turned around an' she sorta jumped on me. She hugged me aroun' the waist. She reached up an' kissed me on the face. She said she never kissed a grown man before an' she might as well kiss me. She says for me to kiss her back.

(Tom *shakes his head with his eyes closed, as he reacts to this ordeal.*)

And I said, Miss Mayella, let me outta here, an' I tried to run, when Mr. Ewell cussed at me from the window an' says he's gonna kill her.

Atticus. And what happened after that?

Tom. I was runnin' so fast, I don't know what happened.

Atticus. Tom, did you rape Mayella Ewell?

Tom. I did not, Sir.

Atticus. Did you harm her in any way?

Tom. I . . . I did not, Sir.

(Atticus *turns and walks to his desk.* Gilmer *rises and goes to the witness chair.*)

Gilmer. Robinson, you're pretty good at bustin' up chifforobes and kindlin' with one hand, aren't you? Strong enough to choke the breath out of a woman and sling her to the floor?

Tom (*meekly*). I never done that, Sir.

Gilmer. But you're strong enough to.

Tom. I reckon so, Sir.

Gilmer. Uh huh. How come you're so all-fired anxious to do that woman's chores?

(Tom *hesitates. He searches for an answer.*)

Tom. Looks like she didn't have nobody to help her. Like I said . . .

Gilmer. With Mr. Ewell and seven children on the place? You did all this choppin' and work out of sheer goodness, boy? You're a mighty good fella, it seems. Did all that for not one penny.

Tom. Yes, Sir. I felt right sorry for her. She seemed . . .

Gilmer. You felt sorry for her? A white woman? You felt sorry for her?

(Tom *realizes his mistake. He shifts uncomfortably in his chair.*)

> Atticus *rises and walks toward the jury.*
> *They watch with no show of emotion. As*
> Atticus *talks, he looks into the eyes of the*
> *men of the jury as if to find one to*
> *encourage him.*

Atticus. To begin with, this case should never have
come to trial. The State has not produced one iota
of medical evidence that the crime Tom Robinson
is charged with ever took place. It has relied instead
on the testimony of two witnesses . . . whose
evidence has not only been called into serious
question on cross-examination, but has been flatly
contradicted by the defendant. There is
circumstantial evidence to indicate that Mayella
Ewell was beaten savagely by someone who led
almost exclusively with his left. And Tom
Robinson now sits before you having taken the
oath with his right hand, the only good hand he
possesses. I have nothing but pity in my heart for
the chief witness for the State. She is a victim of
cruel poverty and ignorance. But my pity does not
extend so far as to her putting a man's life at stake,
which she has done in an effort to get rid of her
own guilt. Now, I say guilt, gentlemen, because it
was guilt that motivated her. She has committed no
crime, she has merely broken a rigid and time-
honored code of our society. A code so severe that
whoever breaks it is hounded from our midst as
unfit to live with. She must destroy the evidence of
her offense. But what was the evidence of her
offense? Tom Robinson, a human being. She must
put Tom Robinson away from her. Tom Robinson
was for her a daily reminder of what she did. And
what did she do? She tempted a Negro. She was
white, and she tempted a Negro. She did something

that in our society is unspeakable. She kissed a black man. Not an old uncle, but a strong, young Negro man. No code mattered to her before she broke it, but it came crashing down on her afterwards. The witnesses for the State, with the exception of the Sheriff of Maycomb County, have presented themselves to you gentlemen, to this court, in the cynical confidence that their testimony would not be doubted. Confident that you gentlemen would go along with them on the assumption, the evil assumption, that all Negroes lie, that all Negroes are basically immoral beings, all Negro men are not to be trusted around our women. An assumption one associates with minds of their caliber, and which is in itself, gentlemen, a lie, which I do not need to point out to you. And so, a quiet, humble, respectable Negro, who has had the unmitigated temerity to feel sorry for a white woman, has had to put his word against two white people. The defendant is not guilty, but somebody in this courtroom is. Now, gentlemen, in this country our courts are the great levelers, and in our courts all men are created equal.

(*The faces of the men of the jury haven't changed expression. Atticus' face begins to perspire. He wipes it with a handkerchief.*)

I'm no idealist to believe firmly in the integrity of our courts and in the jury system. That is no ideal to me. It is a living, working reality. Now I am confident that you gentlemen will review without passion the evidence that you have heard, come to a decision, and restore this man to his family. In the name of God, do your duty. In the name of God, believe Tom Robinson.

(Atticus *turns away from the jury. He walks and sits down next to* Tom *at the table.*)

INTERIOR: BALCONY OF COURTROOM—SEVERAL HOURS LATER. NIGHT.

> Jem *is leaning on the rail of the balcony.* Reverend Sykes *is behind him, with* Dill *sleeping next to him. The* Reverend *fans himself with his hat.*

Jem. How long has the jury been out now, Reverend?

Sykes. Let's see . . . (*He pulls out his pocket watch and looks at it.*) Almost two hours now.

Jem. I think that's an awful good sign, don't you?

(Reverend Sykes *doesn't answer him.*)

INTERIOR: COURTROOM. NIGHT.

> The jury *comes back into the courtroom.* Tom *is brought in and walks toward* Atticus. *The jailer unlocks the handcuffs from* Tom. Tom *sits next to* Atticus. *The* Bailiff *enters the courtroom, followed by the* Judge.

Bailiff. Court's now in session. Everybody rise.

(*The group in the courtroom rises. The* Judge *climbs to his chair and sits down. The spectators are then seated.*)

Judge. Gentlemen of the jury, have you reached a verdict?

Foreman. We have, your honor.

Judge. Will the defendant please rise and face the jury.

(Tom Robinson *rises and faces the jury.*)

What is your verdict?

Foreman. We find the defendant guilty as charged.

(Tom *sits down beside* Atticus.)

Judge. Gentlemen, this jury is dismissed.

Bailiff. Court's adjourned.

(*The* Judge *rises and exits through the door. The crowd murmurs and begins to disperse. The jailer moves to* Tom *and puts handcuffs on him.* Atticus *walks with* Tom.)

Atticus. I'll go to see Helen first thing in the morning. I told her not to be disappointed, we'd probably lose this time.

(Tom *looks at him but doesn't answer.*)

Tom . . .

(Atticus *turns from the door and walks to his table. He starts to gather up the papers on his desk. He puts them in his briefcase. He starts to leave the courtroom. He walks down the middle aisle. Scout is leaning over the rail watching her father and the people below. As* Atticus *walks down the aisle, the Negroes in the balcony start to rise until all are standing. Scout is so busy watching* Atticus *that she isn't aware of this. Reverend Sykes taps her on the shoulder.*)

Sykes. Miss Jean Louise . . . Miss Jean Louise.

(Scout *looks around.*)

Miss Jean Louise, stand up, your father's passin'.

(Scout *rises. The* Reverend *puts his arm around her. Everyone in the colored balcony remains standing until* Atticus *exits out the courtroom door.*)

EXTERIOR: MISS MAUDIE'S PORCH. NIGHT.

> Miss Maudie *is alone on her porch. She
> sees* Atticus *and the children coming
> down the sidewalk. She goes out to her
> yard.* Atticus *and the children come up to
> her.*

Maudie. Atticus . . . (*The children go to the porch and sit
down.*) I . . . I'm sorry, Atticus.

Atticus. Well, thank you, Maudie.

(*A car comes down the road and stops in front of* Miss
Maudie's *house.* Heck Tate *is at the wheel.*)

Tate. Atticus, can I see you for a minute?

Atticus. Would you excuse me?

(Maudie *nods, and* Atticus *moves to the car and talks to*
Tate. Maudie *sits next to* Jem *on the steps.*)

Maudie. Jem.

Jem. Yes'm.

Maudie. I don't know if it'll help, but I want to say
this to you. There are some men in this world who
were born to do our unpleasant jobs for us. Your
father's one of them.

(Heck Tate *drives off.* Atticus *stands quietly for a moment
and then walks back to the steps.*)

What's the matter, Atticus?

Atticus. Tom Robinson's dead. They were taking him
to Abbottsville for safekeeping. Tom broke loose
and ran. The deputy called out to him to stop. Tom
didn't stop. He shot at him to wound him and
missed his aim. Killed him. The deputy says Tom
just ran like a crazy man. The last thing I told him

was not to lose heart, that we'd ask for an appeal. We had such a good chance. We had more than a good chance. I have to go out and tell his family. Would you look after the children, Maudie?

Jem (*starting after him*). Atticus, you want me to go with you?

Atticus. No Son, I think I'd better go out there alone.

Jem (*still going after him*). Atticus, Atticus, I'm goin' with you.

Atticus. All right, Son.

(*He waits for* Jem *to catch up to him.* Maudie, Dill, *and* Scout *stay huddled together on the steps watching them go.* Atticus *drives the car out of the garage and they go off.*)

EXTERIOR: TOM ROBINSON'S HOUSE. NIGHT.

> *The house is dark and quiet, as are all the little houses near it.* Atticus *drives the car in and shines the headlights on the porch of the house where the* Robinson *family is seated and standing, talking.* Spence, *Tom's father, sits on the steps of the house.* Atticus *and* Jem *drive up to the house.* Atticus *stops the car and gets out.* Spence *sees who it is and comes to him.*

Spence. Hello, Mr. Finch. I'm Spence, Tom's father.

(*They shake hands.*)

Atticus. Hello, Spence. Is Helen here?

Spence. Yes Sir. She's inside, lyin' down, tryin' to get a little sleep. We been talkin' about the appeal, Mr. Finch. How long do you think it'll take?

Atticus. Spence, there isn't going to be any appeal now. Tom is dead.

(Helen Robinson *comes out of the front door. They all move toward her.* Atticus *takes off his hat.*)

Helen . . .

(Helen *gives a little moan and falls over into the dirt of the yard.* Spence *and* Atticus *go to her. They lift her. She is crying. They half-carry her into the house as the others watch.*)

(Bob Ewell *comes up the road and stands near Atticus' car. He calls to one of the Negro children in the yard.* Jem *watches from inside the car.*)

Ewell. Boy, go inside and tell Atticus Finch I said to come out here. Go on, boy.

(*The boy goes inside the house.* Ewell *stands in front of the car. He turns and looks at* Jem. Atticus *comes out of the house and stands on the porch. He walks down the steps, past the Negroes, and goes to* Ewell *and stands in front of him.* Ewell *spits in Atticus' face.* Atticus *stares at him, wipes off his face, and starts to get into the car. He and* Jem *drive off as* Ewell *watches them angrily.*)

EXTERIOR: FINCH HOUSE. NIGHT. AUTUMN.

Jean Louise (*voice over*). By October, things had settled down again. I still looked for Boo every time I went by the Radley place.

(Scout *is walking on the sidewalk by the picket fence. She turns and runs to the house.*)

INTERIOR: SCOUT'S BEDROOM.

She comes in and takes her Halloween costume.

Jean Louise (*voice over*). This night my mind was filled with Halloween. There was to be a pageant representing our county's agricultural products.

EXTERIOR: HOUSE. NIGHT.

> Scout, *in her Halloween costume, comes out followed by* Jem.
>
> *Moving shot. They walk to the school building, past carriages and cars parked on the street. They exit into the building.*

Jean Louise (*voice over*). I was to be a ham. Jem said he would escort me to the school auditorium. Thus began our longest journey together.

EXTERIOR: SCHOOLHOUSE. NIGHT.

> *The carriages and cars are now gone.* Jem *is seated on the steps of the schoolhouse. He gets up, walks up the steps to open the door, and looks inside.*

Jem. Scout.

Scout (*off camera*). Yeah.

Jem. Will you come on. Everybody's gone.

Scout (*off camera*). I can't go home like this.

Jem. Well, I'm goin'. It's almost ten o'clock and Atticus will be waitin' for us.

(*He turns and comes down the steps.*)

Scout (*off camera*). All right. I'm comin'.

(*He turns and looks as* Scout *comes out of the door with her ham costume on.*)

But I feel like a fool walkin' home like this.

Jem. Well, it's not my fault that you lost your dress.

Scout. I didn't lose it. Just can't find it.

(She comes down the steps to Jem.)

Jem. Where are your shoes?

Scout. Can't find them either.

Jem. You can get 'em tomorrow.

Scout. But tomorrow is Sunday.

Jem. You can get the janitor to let you in. Come on.

(They start out.)

(Moving shot. They walk into the wooded area. Jem stoops down and picks up sticks and hits trees with them as they walk along. It is black dark out there.)

Here, Scout, let me hold onto you before you break your neck. *(Takes her hand as they walk.)*

Scout. Jem, you don't have to hold me.

Jem. Sshhhh.

Scout. What's the matter?

Jem. Hush a minute, Scout. *(Moves and looks to his right.)* Thought I heard somethin'. Ah, come on. *(They go about five paces when he makes her stop again.)* Wait.

Scout. Jem, are you tryin' to scare me?

Jem. Sshhh.

(There is stillness except for the breathing of the children. Far away a dog howls.)

Scout. You know I'm too old.

Jem. Be quiet.

Scout. I heard an old dog then.

Jem. It's not that. I hear it when we're walking along. When we stop, I don't hear it any more.

Scout. You hear my costume rustlin'. Halloween's got you. (*Moves and then stops.*) I hear it now.

(*The two of them stand still and listen.*)

I'll bet it's just old Cecil Jacobs tryin' to scare us. (*She yells.*) Cecil Jacobs is a big wet hen.

(*There is not a sound except the word "hen" reverberating.*)

Jem. Come on.

(*Scout and Jem start walking. Jem looks frightened. He holds his hand on Scout's head, covered by the ham costume. More than a rustle is heard now. Footsteps are heard, as if someone were walking behind them in heavy shoes. Jem presses Scout's head. They stop to listen. They can hear someone running toward them.*)

Run, Scout!

(*She takes a big step and she reels; she can't keep her balance in the dark. A form descends on her and grabs her, and she falls to the ground and rolls. From nearby, she can hear scuffling, kicking sounds, sounds of shoes and flesh scraping dirt and root. Jem rolls against her and is up like lightning, pulling Scout with him, but she is so entangled by the costume they can't get very far.*)

Run, Scout!

(*They are nearly to the road when Jem's hand leaves her. There is more scuffling and a dull crunching sound, and Scout screams. The scuffling slowly dies away and then there is silence. She can see a man now. He groans and is pulling something heavy along the ground. The man walks away from her, heavily and unsteadily, toward the road.*)

(*She makes her way to where she thinks the road is.*)

(Scout's *point of view. She looks down the road to the street light. A man passes under it. He is carrying the limp body of* Jem. *The man continues on, crosses the Finch yard. The front door opens and* Atticus *runs down the steps.*)

(*Back to* Scout *as she runs to him, and he picks her up.*)

Atticus. What happened? What happened?

Scout. I swear, I don't know. I just don't know.

(Calpurnia *comes out of the door.* Atticus *turns and carries* Scout *up the steps.*)

Atticus. You go and tell Dr. Reynolds to come over.

Calpurnia. Yes Sir.

INTERIOR: JEM'S ROOM. NIGHT.

> Atticus *enters with* Scout. *He puts* Scout *down in the front of* Jem's *room.* Jem *is lying on the bed.*

Atticus. You all right?

Scout. Yes Sir.

Atticus. Are you sure?

Scout. Yes Sir.

(Atticus *rises and leaves the room.* Scout *turns and looks at* Jem *lying on the bed.*)

INTERIOR: HALL. NIGHT.

> Atticus goes *to the phone.* Scout *runs to* Atticus.

Atticus. Sheriff Tate, please.

Scout. Atticus, is Jem dead?

Atticus. No, he's unconscious. We won't know how bad he's hurt until the doctor gets here. (*Talking on the phone.*) Heck? Atticus Finch. Someone's been after my children.

INTERIOR: JEM'S ROOM. NIGHT.

> *Jem's door is slightly open.* Calpurnia *opens the door all the way for* Dr. Reynolds. Atticus *and* Scout *are there.* Dr. Reynolds *enters and examines* Jem.

Dr. Reynolds. He's got a bad break, so far as I can tell, like somebody tried to wring his arm off. I'll be right back, Atticus.

EXTERIOR: PORCH. NIGHT.

> Dr. Reynolds *goes out of the front door.* Tate *comes on the porch with the ham costume.*

Tate. How's the boy, Doc?

Dr. Reynolds. He'll be all right.

INTERIOR: JEM'S ROOM. NIGHT.

> Tate *is at the door of Jem's room. The room is dim. Jem's reading light is shaded with a towel.* Jem *lies on his back, asleep. There is an ugly mark on the side of his face. His left arm is out from the side of his body. The man who brought* Jem *stands in a corner, leaning against the wall.* Atticus *is by* Jem's *bed.* Scout *and* Heck Tate *come in.*

Atticus. What is it, Heck?

(Tate *runs his hands down his thighs. He looks around the room.*)

Tate. Bob Ewell's lyin' on the ground under that tree down yonder with a kitchen knife stuck up under his ribs. He's dead, Mr. Finch.

(Atticus *gets up from the bed. He looks shocked.*)

Atticus. Are you sure?

Tate. Yes Sir. He ain't gonna bother these children no more. Miss Scout, you think you could tell us what happened?

(Scout *goes to* Atticus. *He puts his arms around her.*)

Scout. I don't know. All of a sudden somebody grabbed me. Knocked me down on the ground. Jem found me there and then Mr. Ewell, I reckon, grabbed him again, and Jem hollered. Then somebody grabbed me. Mr. Ewell, I guess. Somebody grabbed him, and then I heard someone pantin' and coughin'. Then I saw someone carrying Jem.

Tate. Well, who was it?

Scout. Why, there he is, Mr. Tate. He can tell you his name . . .

(*She points to the man in the corner who brought* Jem *home. He leans against the wall. He has a pale face and his hair is thin and dead white, and as she points to him, a strange spasm shakes him. At this moment, it comes to* Scout *who he is, and she gazes at him in wonder as a timid smile comes to his face.*)

Hey, Boo.

Atticus. Miss Jean Louise, Mr. Arthur Radley. I believe he already knows you.

(Scout *is embarrassed and tries to hide her embarrassment. She goes to cover* Jem *up.*)

Heck, let's go out on the front porch.

(Atticus *and* Tate *start out the door.* Scout *walks to* Boo, *standing in the corner behind the door.*)

Scout. Would you like to say good night to Jem, Mr. Arthur?

(*She holds out her hand and he takes it.* Jem *is lying in bed asleep as* Boo *and* Scout *walk to the bed.*)

You can pet him, Mr. Arthur. He's asleep. Couldn't if he was awake, though. He wouldn't let you.

(Boo *looks down at* Jem.)

Go ahead.

(*He bends down, and his hand reaches out and pats* Jem, *asleep in bed. Then he withdraws his hand from* Jem's *head. He straightens up, still looking down at* Jem. Scout *takes* Boo *by the hand.*)

EXTERIOR: FINCH PORCH. NIGHT.

> Scout, *holding Boo's hand, opens the door and they both come out on the porch.* Atticus *and* Tate *are there.*

Scout. Let's sit in the swing, Mr. Arthur.

(Scout *and* Boo *walk to the swing and they sit down in it.*)

Atticus. Heck, I guess that the thing to do is . . . good Lord, I must be losing my memory. I can't remember whether Jem is twelve or thirteen. Anyway, it'll have to come before the County Court. Of course, it's a clear case of self-defense. I'll . . . well . . . I'll run down to the office . . .

Tate. Mr. Finch, you think Jem killed Bob Ewell? Is that what you think? Your boy never stabbed him.

(Atticus *looks up.* Boo *and* Scout *are seated in the swing.* Scout *looks up at* Boo.)

Bob Ewell fell on his knife. He killed himself. There's a black man dead for no reason, and now the man responsible for it is dead. Let the dead bury the dead this time, Mr. Finch. I never heard tell that it's against the law for a citizen to do his utmost to prevent a crime from being committed, which is exactly what he did. But maybe you'll tell me it's my duty to tell the town all about it, not to hush it up. Well, you know what'll happen then. All the ladies in Maycomb, includin' my wife, will be knockin' on his door bringin' angel food cakes. To my way of thinkin', takin' one man who's done you and this town a great service, and draggin' him, with his shy ways, into the limelight, to me, that's a sin. It's a sin, and I'm not about to have it on my head. I may not be much, Mr. Finch, but I'm still Sheriff of Maycomb County, and Bob Ewell fell on his knife.

(Atticus *looks over at* Boo. Tate's *meaning dawns on him.*)

Good night, Sir.

(Tate *goes down the steps of the porch and to his car.* Scout *and* Boo *are still seated in the swing.* Scout *gets up and walks over to* Atticus.)

Scout. Mr. Tate was right.

Atticus. What do you mean?

Scout. Well, it would be sort of like shooting a mockingbird, wouldn't it?

(Atticus *hugs her to him.* Boo *walks over to Jem's window, bends over, and looks inside.* Atticus *walks over to* Boo *at the window. They shake hands.*)

Atticus. Thank you, Arthur. Thank you for my children.

(Atticus *turns and walks into the house.* Boo *and* Scout *go off the porch.*)

(*Moving shot. They walk along the sidewalk. They turn in at the Radley gate and go up the front walk.*)

Jean Louise (*voice over*). Neighbors bring food with death, and flowers with sickness, and little things in between. Boo was our neighbor. He gave us two soap dolls, a broken watch and chain, a knife, and our lives.

(*They go up the steps and onto the porch to the front door.* Boo *opens the door and goes inside.*)

One time Atticus said you never really knew a man until you stood in his shoes and walked around in them. Just standin' on the Radley porch was enough.

(*Moving shot.* Scout *turns and walks down the steps of the porch.*)

The summer that had begun so long ago had ended, another summer had taken its place, and a fall, and Boo Radley had come out.

(Scout *turns at the gate and looks back at the house. She turns and goes down the walk.*)

I was to think of these days many times; of Jem, and Dill, and Boo Radley, and Tom Robinson . . .

INTERIOR: JEM'S ROOM. NIGHT.

> Atticus *and* Scout *are inside Jem's room on Jem's bed.*

. . . and Atticus. He would be in Jem's room all night. And he would be there when Jem waked up in the morning.

FADE OUT.

RELATED READINGS

from Growing Up in the Great Depression

by Richard Wormser

This excerpt explains the stock market crash of 1929 and the Great Depression and describes their impacts on the nation. Think about how these historic events might have affected small southern towns such as Maycomb, Alabama.

In 1930 America went bust. A great economic depression settled over the country like a plague, afflicting the rich and the poor, men, women, and children, black and white, foreign- and native-born, workers and farmers. Millions of people lost their jobs, their businesses, their farms, their homes, their savings, and their self-respect.

It all seemed to happen suddenly. For ten years the country seemed to be on a spending spree. In 1920, 7.5 million automobiles had been purchased. By 1929 there were 26.5 million. The sales of goods rose from $4.9 billion in 1920 to $7.06 billion in 1929. Industry was booming. From 1925 to 1929, the number of factories increased from 183,877 to 206,663. More high school students were graduating than ever before (from 16 percent in 1920 to 28 percent in 1930).

With money came the pursuit of pleasure. The 1920s were a decade of fads: the crossword puzzle, golf, and a Chinese game called Mah-Jongg. Everybody seemed to be out for a good time. The dance crazes were the Charleston and the Black Bottom. People flocked to the theater to watch glamorous shows and show girls. And while it was illegal to buy or sell liquor (a constitutional amendment had been passed in 1918 that banned alcoholic beverages), there was plenty of "booze" around. The gangsters and bootleggers made sure of that. Al Capone and "Bugs" Moran owned Chicago, Dutch Schultz and Arnold Rothstein ruled New York, the Purple Gang controlled Detroit, while Joe Kennedy, the father of the future president of the United States, was a major bootleg liquor dealer in Boston. Not only did bootleggers supply people with liquor, they supplied the places in which to drink it. They opened clubs and speakeasies where you could dance, drink, and often gamble without fear of arrest because the police had been paid off. It was no wonder preachers were warning that America was on the road to hell. They were far more accurate than most people gave them credit for.

The index of America's prosperity was Wall Street and the stock market. From the end of World War I in 1919 stock prices kept rising. In 1924, the average price of the twenty-five leading industrial stocks in America was $120 a share. By 1929, the same stocks were worth $542. Many people believed they had found a money machine that could not fail. Everybody knew somebody—or so they said—who had bought a stock at $10 one day and sold it for $20 the next. And the person who bought it for $20 sold it for $50—and so on down the line. It seemed as if prosperity would last forever. One of the famous millionaires of the day, Jacob Raskob, remarked, "Not only can one be rich, but one ought to be rich."

Despite the fact that millions were being made on the stock market, most Americans lacked money to invest. Out of the then 27.5 million families in America, 21.5 million of them earned under $3,000 a year, and, of those, 6 million families earned less than $1,000.

Yet advertising told them that they too had a role to play in the general prosperity. They were urged to buy the goods and services the society was producing.

from *Growing Up in the Great Depression*   85

Most people bought, but many couldn't afford to pay the full price all at once. Instead, they bought on credit. They bought cars on credit, clothes on credit, houses on credit, furniture on credit, radios on credit. And the more goods they bought, the more were manufactured for them to buy, and the higher the stock market rose.

But underneath the glitter, there were distinct rumblings of an economic earthquake, and many of the "big boys"—which was what the newspapers called the most influential business leaders—knew it. Publicly, they were making statements declaring the stock market to be solid and urging people to buy stocks and invest in America. Privately they were selling all the stocks they owned. The insiders knew that many businesses were having hard times. Despite the seeming prosperity, unemployment in certain industries was high, farm prices were low, and stocks were selling for much more than they were worth. Even Herbert Hoover, who was then president of the United States, knew it. But the stock market was riding on a speeding roller coaster and the president's men were afraid that if they tried to control it, the roller coaster would fly off the tracks and injure a lot of people. So they did nothing, hoping that everything would work itself out.

On October 24, 1929, the roller coaster finally crashed. Stock prices plummeted. The more desperate people were to get rid of their stocks, the lower prices fell. On that one day, the value of stocks fell fourteen billion dollars. Everybody wanted to sell, but nobody wanted to buy. There seemed to be no end to the slide. Prices for stocks and bonds dropped hour by hour. Thousands of small investors watched the stock market quotations appear on the ticker tape, the numbers lower each time they passed by. People crowded around radio rooms on ocean liners, in newspaper offices, and made long distance calls one after another to hear the news. On the floor of the stock exchange, there was total confusion and then panic. Brokers physically battled one another to compete for the few buyers available. They pulled one another's hair, bit, punched, and shoved in order to make a sale—and at any price. A messenger boy who happened to be at the stock exchange by chance offered a bid of one dollar as a joke for shares in White Sewing Machine and wound up owning ten thousand shares of stock in the company.

The captains of industry and finance as well as President Hoover kept making public statements that the crash was temporary. But prices continued to fall. Within a year, the sale of railroad and utility bonds dropped from $10 billion to $1 billion. The average income per person dropped from $847 a year to $465. Millions of investors were financially ruined, losing everything they owned. They had bought stocks on margin, which meant that they actually paid for only a small part of the stock's value and owed the rest, assuming they could pay it off as the stock price rose. Now they were being called to put up the rest of the money. They exhausted their savings, sold their wives' jewelry, borrowed from friends and relatives, trying to raise cash to cover their losses. It was like throwing money down a bottomless well.

A few committed suicide. When the president of a cigar company saw the value of stock in his company drop from $113.50 to $4 a share in a single day, he rented a hotel room, climbed out on the ledge, and, despite the efforts of a waiter to drag him back inside, jumped to his death. Another man, having lost all his money and owing hundreds of thousands, shot himself. His dying words were, "Tell the boys I can't pay." Many who killed themselves did so because the crash exposed their illegal dealings. Bank presidents were caught using customers' money to play the market. Rumors of suicides became so exaggerated that when a man was spotted working on a roof of a building, a crowd gathered to see if he would jump. In a few tragic cases, ruined men went home and killed their families before killing themselves. The economic lights had gone out and there was darkness throughout the land.

What caused the Great Depression? Some said the wealth of the country was badly distributed: too many rich people and too many poor. The top 5 percent of the country owned 33 percent of all the real wealth. The 27,400 wealthiest families had as much money as the 12 million poorest families. The poor had no money to buy goods and services, so after a while there were too many products on the market and not enough people to buy them. The taxes on imports from other countries were so high that foreigners couldn't sell their goods here and make money to pay their debts to the United States. In addition, the foundations on which many businesses were built were shaky. Many companies' stock had risen to a lot more than the companies were really worth. At the first tremors, these firms went broke. It was like a snowball rolling downhill, getting bigger and rolling faster every second. When the companies went broke, so did the banks that had lent them money. Workers who lost their jobs couldn't pay their bills. The businesses that depended upon them also went under because they didn't have enough customers to survive. When the snowball finally came to a stop, there was one vast heap of ruined companies, ruined factories, ruined banks, and ruined human lives. A nurse in Tucson, Arizona, wrote:

> I retired one night safe and independent with $7852.00 in the bank and awoke the next morning with $12.00 in my purse. Like so many others, I lost all my savings in a bank failure.

And a man in Florida wrote the president:

> Is there no department to take care of the injustice done to me who bought stocks instead of a home? Mine was not paper money but hard earned dollars. I have worked hard and long and now I have not enough money to pay a necessary dentist's bill. I was born with a sense of justice and now it has been outraged.

In October 1931, two years after the collapse of the stock market, 9,378,000 workers were unemployed. In December, 10,814,000 were out of work. In January of 1932, unemployment grew to 11,500,000. In March, it rose to 12,000,000 and in June, 13,000,000. By December it was 13,587,000. In January 1933 it reached 14,597,000, and in March, when Franklin Delano Roosevelt was inaugurated as president of the United States, unemployment had reached 15,071,000. In some cities, 80 percent of the work force was without jobs. At the lowest point in the depression, 34 million men, women, and children were without income, 28 percent of the American people. Factories were working at 15 percent of capacity, if they were working at all. More than 6,000 banks went bankrupt, one-quarter of the nation's banks; 85,000 businesses had failed. The price of wheat dropped from $1.09 to 39 cents a bushel. Farmers in the Midwest burned their crops and poured milk onto the highways to protest the fact that the prices they would receive from selling the food was far less than the cost of raising and transporting it.

Hundreds of thousands of people were evicted from their homes and farms and lived in tents and shacks made of cardboard, tar paper, scrap wood, or metal. Fewer people got married and fewer children were born. By 1932, more than a million children were not receiving an education because there was no money to pay teachers. Some schools were operating only three days a week and others closed ten months of the year. There was some relief for the needy from local governments and charities, but to be eligible, people had to sell their possessions, including their home, and cancel their life insurance. Some states would not allow people on relief to vote and some churches banned families on relief from attending services. There was talk of revolution in the air. Hitler had come to power in Germany, and there were those who admired him. Stalin was in power in the Soviet Union, and there were those who believed that he had the answer.

People turned their eyes and hopes to the government for help. The president, Herbert Hoover, was an able administrator, but he lacked compassion. He believed that the federal government shouldn't interfere in the crisis, that depressions were natural and normal under capitalism, and that things would soon get better. "The traditional business of the country is . . . on a sound and prosperous basis," he said. When a few thousand World War I veterans peacefully marched to Washington to pressure Congress to give them a bonus promised to them for 1945, Hoover used federal troops against them. The soldiers drove the veterans out with bayonets and tanks and burned their makeshift homes, even though the demonstrators were unarmed. When farmers and workers sought economic help from the government, Hoover denied it to them. He did, however, make money available to certain big businesses to keep them afloat. People were so angry with him that they called the colonies of makeshift houses built by the homeless "Hoovervilles" as an expression of their contempt for the president. By 1932 it had become clear that Herbert Hoover was no longer the American people's choice for the job.

The man the people turned to was Franklin Delano Roosevelt. One-time vice presidential candidate, former governor of New York, crippled by polio and confined to a wheelchair, Roosevelt was a man of remarkable spirit and temperament. In spite of being a nephew of former president Theodore Roosevelt and born to a life of wealth and privilege, Roosevelt had an intuitive empathy with most of the American people. He inspired them and gave them hope. In turn, they loved and trusted him, and in their despair turned to him for salvation.

Elected by a landslide in 1932, Roosevelt set the tone of his administration in his inauguration speech in March of 1933. As the nation listened to him over the radio, he spoke the following words of inspiration:

> Let me first assert my firm belief that the only thing we have to fear is fear itself. Nameless, unreasoning, unjustified terror which paralyzes needed efforts to convert retreat into advance.

But despite Roosevelt's speech and his policies, which would profoundly change the relationship between the federal government and the people, the depression lasted ten long, hard years.

The Right Thing to Do at the Time

by George Garrett

Like Atticus Finch, the lawyer in this story stands on his own principles, even if they go against the ideals and laws of the town.

This is a true story about my father, a true story with the shape of a piece of fiction. Well, why not? Where do you suppose all the shapes and forms of fiction came from in the first place? And what's the purpose of fiction anyway, whether it's carved out of the knotty hardwood of personal experience or spun out of the slick thin air like soap bubbles? "What's the purpose of the bayonet?" they used to yell when I was a soldier years ago. The correct answer was: "To kill, *to kill,* TO KILL!"

The purpose of fiction is simply to tell the truth.

My father was a small-town southern lawyer, not a writer, but he was a truth-teller. And he would tell the truth, come what may, hell or high water. And since he loved the truth and would gladly risk his life (and ours, the whole family's) for the sake of it, he would fight without stint, withholding nothing, offering no pity or quarter against what he took to be wrong— that is, against the untruth. He would go to any length he had to. And that is what this story is all about— how far one man would go to fight for the truth and against what was and is wrong.

We were living in the cow town of Kissimmee, Florida, in the early years of the Great Depression. Disney World is near there now, and it looks pretty much like everyplace else. But it was a hard, tough place then, a place where life was hard for many decent people, black and white. And it was a place where some not-so-decent people had managed to seize power and to hold power and were extremely unlikely to be dislodged from power. Among the people in power in those days were the Ku Klux Klan, not a sad little bunch of ignorant racists in bedsheets but a real clan, a native-grown kind of organized crime family.

My father and his law partner were fighting against the Klan in court and in public with the promise that they would (as they, in fact, did) represent free of charge any person at all who chose to resist the Klan and wanted a lawyer.

This exposed position led to a whole lot of trouble, believe me. And in the end it led to the demise of the Klan as a power of any kind in central Florida. But the big trouble came later. This happened early on as the lines were being drawn and the fight was just getting under way.

Sometimes in the early evening we would go together, my mother and father and the other children, into town for an ice-cream cone: a great treat in those days. One evening we piled into our old car and drove into the center of town and parked in front of the drugstore. Went inside and sat on tall swivel chairs at the counter eating our ice-cream cones. We were all sitting there in a row when a young policeman walked in. Try as I will, I can't remember his name anymore. Just that he was very young and that my mother, who was a teacher then, had taught him in high school. He greeted her politely at first. He seemed a little awkward and embarrassed.

"Mr. Garrett," he said to my father, "I'm afraid I'm going to have to give you a red ticket."

"Oh really?" my father said, still licking his ice-cream cone. "What for?"

"Well, sir, your tail lights don't work."

"They did when I came down here."

"Well, sir, they sure don't now."

"Let's have a look."

So we all trooped outside and looked at the tail lights. They didn't work, all right, because they were broken and there was shattered red glass all over the street right behind the back bumper.

"I wonder who would do a thing like that," my father said, giving the young cop a hard look.

"Well, I wouldn't know, sir," he said. "I just work for the city and I do what I'm told. And I have to write you a ticket."

"Fine," my father said. "I understand that."

Then he surprised the cop and us too by asking if he could pay for the ticket right then and there. And the cop said yes, that was his legal right, and he said it would cost five dollars.

Now that was considerable money in those days when grown men with some skills were earning eight or ten dollars a week. Nobody had any money in those days, nobody we knew or knew of. Most of my father's clients, those who could pay at all, paid him in produce and fresh eggs, things like that.

My father peeled off five one-dollar bills. The cop wrote him a receipt. Then my father told my mother to drive us on home when we had finished our ice cream. He had to go somewhere right away.

He whistled loudly and waved his arm for a taxi. One came right over from the Atlantic Coastline depot directly across the way. He kissed my mother on the cheek and said he would be back just as soon as he could. Gave her the keys to our car and hopped into the cab.

None of us heard what he told the driver: "Let's go to Tallahassee."

Tallahassee was and is the state capital, a good

three hundred or so miles away by bad, narrow roads in those days.

Much later we learned what happened. They arrived very late. Slept in the cab. First thing in the morning he got himself a shave in the barbershop. Then went to the legislature. Where, exercising a constitutional right to speak on this kind of matter, he quickly established that the town charter for Kissimmee, Florida, was completely illegal and unconstitutional. In a technical, legal sense that town did not exist and never had. It would require a special action of the state legislature to give the town a new charter and a legal existence. Having made his point, he thanked the legislators kindly and left the capitol. Woke the snoring taxi driver and said, "Let's go back home."

It probably cost him a hundred dollars for that ride. Maybe more. He never told us, and nobody, not even my mother, ever dared ask him.

By the time he arrived home there was a delegation waiting to see him at our house: the mayor, the chief of police, the judge, pretty much the whole gang. Legislators had been on the phone all day to them, and they were deeply worried. Because, you see, everything they had ever done, in the absence of a valid town charter, including collecting taxes, had been illegal. You can imagine what that could mean if people got it in mind to be litigious about things.

Everybody came into our living room. And the whole family, too, because, he said, we saw the beginning of it and deserved to see the end.

Before the mayor or any of them said a word, he explained to them exactly what he had done. And he told them that, under the state constitution, establishing a town was a very tricky legal business. He said the chances were a hundred to one that they would mess it up again. He wished them good luck, promising that if they ever bothered him or us anymore, he would go to Tallahassee again and close them down for keeps.

There was a lot of silence. Finally the mayor spoke.

"What do you want from us, Garrett?"

"Ah," said my father. "I knew it would come down to that. And I'm glad it did, because there is something I do want from you all."

They were all looking and waiting. I reckon they were ready to do or pay most anything. That's how things were handled.

"Damn it!" he said. "I want my five dollars back from that phony traffic ticket."

Long pause.

"That's all?"

"That's all. You give me my five dollars back and I'll give you back your receipt."

So they paid him the five dollars and he tore the receipt in two and they filed out of our house.

"You beat them, Daddy," I said. "You won!"

"That's right, boy," he told me. "And I taught them a very important lesson."

"What's that?" my mother asked, nervously.

"If they want to stop me now," he said, "they're going to have to kill me. And I don't think they've got the guts for it."

Then he laughed out loud. And so did I, not because it was funny, but because it seemed like the right thing to do at the time.

Lawyer Clark Blues

by Sleepy John Estes

*What do you think of lawyers? Think
about Tom Robinson's opinion of Atticus
Finch as you read these blues lyrics.*

Now
Got offices in town
Resident out on 70 Road
He got a nice little lake
5   Right inside the grove

> Boys you know I like Mr. Clark
> Yes he really is my friend
> He say if I just stay out of the grave
> He see that I won't go to the pen

10   Now
Mr. Clark is a lawyer
His younger brother is too
When the battle get hot
He tell him just what to do

15
> Boys you know I like Mr. Clark
> Yes you know he is my friend
> He say if I just stay out of the grave
> He see that I won't go to the pen

Now
20   He lawyer for the rich
He lawyer for the poor
He don't try to rob no body
Just bring along a little dough

Boys you know I like Mr. Clark
25 Yes he really is my friend
He say if I just stay out of the grave
He see that I won't go to the pen

Now
Once I got in trouble
30 You know I was gonna take a ride
He didn't let it reach the court house
He kept it on the outside

Boys you know I like Mr. Clark
Yes he really is my friend
35 He say if I just stay out of the graveyard
Old John I see that you won't go to the pen

Now
Mr. Clark is a good lawyer
He good as I ever seen
40 He's the first man that proved that
Water run up stream

Boys you know I like Mr. Clark
Yes he really is my friend
He say if I just stay out of the grave
45 Old John I see you won't go to the pen

Strange Fruit

by Lewis Allan

*One of jazz vocalist Billie Holiday's
signature songs, "Strange Fruit" tells of the
lynchings that were common in the South
at the beginning of the century. Lewis
Allan's song of protest helped to bring
attention to these crimes by sharing the
experience with people throughout the
nation. Some music critics recall that when
the song was first performed, audiences
were not aware of its powerful message
against racial injustice.*

Southern trees bear a strange fruit,
Blood on the leaves and blood at the root,
Black body swinging in the southern breeze,
Strange fruit hanging from the poplar trees.
5 Pastoral scene of the gallant south,
The bulging eyes and the twisted mouth,
Scent of magnolia sweet and fresh,
And the sudden smell of burning flesh!
Here is a fruit for the crows to pluck,
10 For the rain to gather, for the wind to suck,
For the sun to rot, for a tree to drop,
Here is a strange and bitter crop.

The Thanksgiving Visitor

by Truman Capote

*Scout and Jem learn the difficult concept
of justice from Atticus. The boy in this
story learns in a similar way.*

Talk about mean! Odd Henderson was the meanest
human creature in my experience.

And I'm speaking of a twelve-year-old boy, not
some grownup who has had the time to ripen a
naturally evil disposition. At least, Odd was twelve in
1932, when we were both second-graders attending a
small-town school in rural Alabama.

Tall for his age, a bony boy with muddy-red hair
and narrow yellow eyes, he towered over all his
classmates—would have in any event, for the rest of
us were only seven or eight years old. Odd had failed
first grade twice and was now serving his second term
in the second grade. This sorry record wasn't due to
dumbness—Odd was intelligent, maybe cunning is a
better word—but he took after the rest of the
Hendersons. The whole family (there were ten of
them, not counting Dad Henderson, who was a
bootlegger and usually in jail, all scrunched together
in a four-room house next door to a Negro church)
was a shiftless, surly bunch, every one of them ready
to do you a bad turn; Odd wasn't the worst of the lot,
and brother, that is *saying* something.

Many children in our school came from families
poorer than the Hendersons; Odd had a pair of shoes,
while some boys, girls too, were forced to go barefoot

right through the bitterest weather—that's how hard the Depression had hit Alabama. But nobody, I don't care who, looked as down-and-out as Odd—a skinny, freckled scarecrow in sweaty cast-off overalls that would have been a humiliation to a chain-gang convict. You might have felt pity for him if he hadn't been so hateful. All the kids feared him, not just us younger kids, but even boys his own age and older.

Nobody ever picked a fight with him except one time a girl named Ann "Jumbo" Finchburg, who happened to be the other town bully. Jumbo, a sawed-off but solid tomboy with an all-hell-let-loose wrestling technique, jumped Odd from behind during recess one dull morning, and it took three teachers, each of whom must have wished the combatants would kill each other, a good long while to separate them. The result was a sort of draw: Jumbo lost a tooth and half her hair and developed a grayish cloud in her left eye (she never could see clear again); Odd's afflictions included a broken thumb, plus scratch scars that will stay with him to the day they shut his coffin. For months afterward, Odd played every kind of trick to goad Jumbo into a rematch; but Jumbo had gotten her licks and gave him considerable berth. As I would have done if he'd let me; alas, I was the object of Odd's relentless attentions.

Considering the era and locale, I was fairly well off—living, as I did, in a high-ceilinged old country house situated where the town ended and the farms and forests began. The house belonged to distant relatives, elderly cousins, and these cousins, three maiden ladies and their bachelor brother, had taken me under their roof because of a disturbance among my more immediate family, a custody battle that, for involved reasons, had left me stranded in this somewhat eccentric Alabama household. Not that I was unhappy there; indeed, moments of those few years turned out to be the happiest part of an otherwise difficult childhood, mainly because the youngest of the cousins, a woman in her sixties, became my first friend. As she was a child herself (many people thought her less than that, and murmured about her as though she were the twin of poor nice Lester Tucker, who roamed the streets in a sweet daze), she understood children, and understood me absolutely.

Perhaps it was strange for a young boy to have as his best friend an aging spinster, but neither of us had an ordinary outlook or background, and so it was inevitable, in our separate loneliness, that we should come to share a friendship apart. Except for the hours I spent at school, the three of us, me and old Queenie, our feisty little rat terrier, and Miss Sook, as everyone called my friend, were almost always together. We hunted herbs in the woods, went fishing on remote creeks (with dried sugarcane stalks for fishing poles) and gathered curious ferns and greeneries that we transplanted and grew with trailing flourish in tin pails and chamber pots. Mostly, though, our life was lived in the kitchen—a farmhouse kitchen, dominated by a big black wood-burning stove, that was often dark and sunny at the same time.

Miss Sook, sensitive as a shy-lady fern, a recluse who had never traveled beyond the county boundaries, was totally unlike her brother and sisters, the latter being down-to-earth, vaguely masculine ladies who operated a dry-goods store and several other business ventures. The brother, Uncle B., owned a number of cotton farms scattered around the countryside; because he refused to drive a car or endure any contact whatever with mobilized machinery, he rode horseback, jogging all day from one property to another. He was a kind man, though a silent one: he grunted yes or no, and really never opened his mouth except to feed it. At every meal he had the appetite of an Alaskan grizzly after a winter's hibernation, and it was Miss Sook's task to fill him up.

Breakfast was our principal meal; midday dinner, except on Sundays, and supper were casual menus, often composed of leftovers from the morning. These breakfasts, served promptly at 5:30 A.M., were regular stomach swellers. To the present day I retain a nostalgic hunger for those cockcrow repasts of ham and fried chicken, fried pork chops, fried catfish, fried squirrel (in season), fried eggs, hominy grits with gravy, black-eyed peas, collards with collard liquor and cornbread to mush it in, biscuits, pound cake, pancakes and molasses, honey in the comb, homemade jams and jellies, sweet milk, buttermilk, coffee chicory-flavored and hot as Hades.

The cook, accompanied by her assistants, Queenie and myself, rose every morning at four to fire the stove and set the table and get everything started. Rising at that hour was not the hardship it may sound; we were used to it, and anyway we always went to bed as soon as the sun dropped and the birds had settled in the trees. Also, my friend was not as frail as she seemed; though she had been sickly as a child and her shoulders were hunched, she had strong hands and sturdy legs. She could move with sprightly, purposeful speed, the frayed tennis shoes she invariably wore squeaking on the waxed kitchen floor, and her distinguished face, with its delicately clumsy features and beautiful, youthful eyes, bespoke a fortitude that suggested it was more the reward of an interior spiritual shine than the visible surface of mere mortal health.

Nevertheless, depending on the season and the number of hands employed on Uncle B.'s farms, there were sometimes as many as fifteen people sitting down to those dawn banquets; the hands were entitled to one hot meal a day—it was part of their wages.

Supposedly, a Negro woman came in to help wash the dishes, make the beds, clean the house and do the laundry. She was lazy and unreliable but a lifelong friend of Miss Sook's—which meant that my friend would not consider replacing her and simply did the work herself. She chopped firewood, tended a large menagerie of chickens, turkeys and hogs, scrubbed, dusted, mended all our clothes; yet when I came home from school, she was always eager to keep me company—to play a card game named Rook or rush off on a mushroom hunt or have a pillow fight or, as we sat in the kitchen's waning afternoon light, help me with homework.

She loved to pore over my textbooks, the geography atlas especially ("Oh, Buddy," she would say, because she called me Buddy, "just think of it—a lake named Titicaca. That really exists somewhere in the world"). My education was her education, as well. Due to her childhood illness, she had had almost no schooling; her handwriting was a series of jagged eruptions, the spelling a highly personal and phonetic affair. I could already write and read with a smoother assurance than she was capable of (though she managed to "study" one Bible chapter every day, and never missed "Little Orphan Annie" or "The Katzenjammer Kids," comics carried by the Mobile paper). She took a bristling pride in "our" report cards ("Gosh, Buddy! Five A's. Even arithmetic. I didn't dare to hope we'd get an A in arithmetic"). It was a mystery to her why I hated school, why some mornings I wept and pleaded with Uncle B., the deciding voice in the house, to let me stay home.

Of course it wasn't that I hated school; what I hated was Odd Henderson. The torments he contrived! For instance, he used to wait for me in the shadows under a water oak that darkened an edge of the school grounds; in his hand he held a paper sack stuffed with prickly cockleburs collected on his way to school. There was no sense in trying to outrun him, for he was quick as a coiled snake; like a rattler, he struck, slammed me to the ground and, his slitty eyes gleeful, rubbed the burrs into my scalp. Usually a circle of kids ganged around to titter, or pretend to; they didn't really think it funny; but Odd made them nervous and ready to please. Later, hiding in a toilet in the boys' room, I would untangle the burrs knotting my hair; this took forever and always meant missing the first bell.

Our second-grade teacher, Miss Armstrong, was sympathetic, for she suspected what was happening; but eventually, exasperated by my continual tardiness, she raged at me in front of the whole class: "Little mister big britches. What a big head he has! Waltzing in here twenty minutes after the bell. A half hour." Whereupon I lost control; I pointed at Odd Henderson and shouted: "Yell at him. He's the one to blame. The sonofabitch."

I knew a lot of curse words, yet even I was shocked when I heard what I'd said resounding in an awful silence, and Miss Armstrong, advancing toward me clutching a heavy ruler, said, "Hold out your hands, sir. Palms up, sir." Then, while Odd Henderson watched with a small citric smile, she blistered the palms of my hands with her brass-edged ruler until the room blurred.

It would take a page in small print to list the imaginative punishments Odd inflicted, but what I resented and suffered from most was the sense of dour expectations he induced. Once, when he had me pinned against a wall, I asked him straight out what had I done to make him dislike me so much; suddenly he relaxed, let me loose and said, "You're a sissy. I'm just straightening you out." He was right, I was a sissy of sorts, and the moment he said it, I realized there was nothing I could do to alter his judgment, other than toughen myself to accept and defend the fact.

As soon as I regained the peace of the warm kitchen, where Queenie might be gnawing an old dug-up bone and my friend puttering with a piecrust, the weight of Odd Henderson would blessedly slide from my shoulders. But too often at night, the narrow lion eyes loomed in my dreams while his high, harsh voice, pronouncing cruel promises, hissed in my ears.

My friend's bedroom was next to mine; occasionally cries arising from my nightmare upheavals wakened her; then she would come and shake me out of an Odd Henderson coma. "Look," she'd say, lighting a lamp, "you've even scared Queenie. She's shaking." And, "Is it a fever? You're wringing wet. Maybe we ought to call Doctor Stone." But she knew that it wasn't a fever, she knew that it was because of my troubles at school, for I had told and told her how Odd Henderson treated me.

But now I'd stopped talking about it, never mentioned it any more, because she refused to acknowledge that any human could be as bad as I made him out. Innocence, preserved by the absence of experience that had always isolated Miss Sook, left her incapable of encompassing an evil so complete.

"Oh," she might say, rubbing heat into my chilled hands, "he only picks on you out of jealousy. He's not smart and pretty as you are." Or, less jestingly, "The thing to keep in mind, Buddy, is this boy can't help acting ugly; he doesn't know any different. All those Henderson children have had it hard. And you can lay that at Dad Henderson's door. I don't like to say it, but that man never was anything except a mischief and a fool. Did you know Uncle B. horsewhipped him once? Caught him beating a dog and horsewhipped him on the spot. The best thing that ever happened was when they locked him up at State Farm. But I remember Molly Henderson before she married Dad. Just fifteen or sixteen she was, and fresh from somewhere across the river. She worked for Sade Danvers down the road, learning to be a dressmaker. She used to pass here and see me hoeing in the garden—such a polite girl, with lovely red hair, and so appreciative of everything; sometimes I'd give her a bunch of sweet peas or a japonica, and she was always so appreciative. Then she began strolling by arm in arm with Dad Henderson—and him so much older and a perfect rascal, drunk or sober. Well, the Lord must have His reasons. But it's a shame; Molly can't be more than thirty-five, and there she is without a tooth in her head or a dime to her name. Nothing but a houseful of children to feed. You've got to take all that into account, Buddy, and be patient."

Patient! What was the use of discussing it? Finally, though, my friend did comprehend the seriousness of my despair. The realization arrived in a quiet way and was not the outcome of unhappy midnight wakings or pleading scenes with Uncle B. It happened one rainy November twilight when we were sitting alone in the kitchen close by the dying stove fire; supper was over, the dishes stacked, and Queenie was tucked in a rocker, snoring. I could hear my friend's whispery voice weaving under the skipping noise of rain on the roof, but my mind was on my worries and I was not attending, though I was aware that her subject was Thanksgiving, then a week away.

My cousins had never married (Uncle B. had *almost* married, but his fiancée returned the engagement ring when she saw that sharing a house with three very individual spinsters would be part of the bargain); however, they boasted extensive family connections throughout the vicinity: cousins aplenty, and an aunt, Mrs. Mary Taylor Wheelwright, who was one hundred and three years old. As our house was the largest and the most conveniently located, it was traditional for these relations to aim themselves our way every year at Thanksgiving; though there were seldom fewer than thirty celebrants, it was not an onerous chore, because we provided only the setting and an ample number of stuffed turkeys.

The guests supplied the trimmings, each of them contributing her particular specialty: a cousin twice removed, Harriet Parker from Flomaton, made perfect ambrosia, transparent orange slices combined with freshly ground coconut; Harriet's sister Alice usually arrived carrying a dish of whipped sweet potatoes and raisins; the Conklin tribe, Mr. and Mrs. Bill Conklin and their quartet of handsome daughters, always brought a delicious array of vegetables canned during the summer. My own favorite was a cold banana pudding—a guarded recipe of the ancient aunt who, despite her longevity, was still domestically energetic; to our sorrow she took the secret with her when she died in 1934, age one hundred and five (and it wasn't age that lowered the curtain; she was attacked and trampled by a bull in a pasture).

Miss Sook was ruminating on these matters while my mind wandered through a maze as melancholy as the wet twilight. Suddenly I heard her knuckles rap the kitchen table: "Buddy!"

"What?"

"You haven't listened to one word."

"Sorry."

"I figure we'll need five turkeys this year. When I spoke to Uncle B. about it, he said he wanted you to kill them. Dress them, too."

"But *why?*"

"He says a boy ought to know how to do things like that."

Slaughtering was Uncle B.'s job. It was an ordeal for me to watch him butcher a hog or even wring a chicken's neck. My friend felt the same way; neither of us could abide any violence bloodier than swatting flies, so I was taken aback at her casual relaying of this command.

"Well, I won't."

Now she smiled. "Of course you won't. I'll get Bubber or some other colored boy. Pay him a nickel. But," she said, her tone descending conspiratorially, "we'll let Uncle B. believe it was you. Then he'll be pleased and stop saying it's such a bad thing."

"What's a bad thing?"

"Our always being together. He says you ought to have other friends, boys your own age. Well, he's right."

"I don't want any other friend."

"Hush, Buddy. Now hush. You've been real good to me. I don't know what I'd do without you. Just become an old crab. But I want to see you happy, Buddy. Strong, able to go out in the world. And you're never going to until you come to terms with people like Odd Henderson and turn them into friends."

"Him! He's the last friend in the world I want."

"Please, Buddy—invite that boy here for Thanksgiving dinner."

Though the pair of us occasionally quibbled, we never quarreled. At first I was unable to believe she meant her request as something more than a sample of poor-taste humor; but then, seeing that she was serious, I realized, with bewilderment, that we were edging toward a falling-out.

"I thought you were my *friend.*"

"I am, Buddy. Truly."

"If you were, you couldn't think up a thing like that. Odd Henderson hates me. He's my *enemy.*"

"He can't hate you. He doesn't know you."

"Well, I hate him."

"Because you don't know him. That's all I ask. The chance for you to know each other a little. Then I think this trouble will stop. And maybe you're right,

Buddy, maybe you boys won't ever be friends. But I doubt that he'd pick on you any more."

"You don't understand. You've never hated anybody."

"No, I never have. We're allotted just so much time on earth, and I wouldn't want the Lord to see me wasting mine in any such manner."

"I won't do it. He'd think I was crazy. And I would be."

The rain had let up, leaving a silence that lengthened miserably. My friend's clear eyes contemplated me as though I were a Rook card she was deciding how to play; she maneuvered a salt-pepper lock of hair off her forehead and sighed. "Then *I* will. Tomorrow," she said, "I'll put on my hat and pay a call on Molly Henderson." This statement certified her determination, for I'd never known Miss Sook to plan a call on anyone, not only because she was entirely without social talent, but also because she was too modest to presume a welcome. "I don't suppose there will be much Thanksgiving in their house. Probably Molly would be very pleased to have Odd sit down with us. Oh, I know Uncle B. would never permit it, but the nice thing to do is invite them all."

My laughter woke Queenie; and after a surprised instant, my friend laughed too. Her cheeks pinked and a light flared in her eyes; rising, she hugged me and said, "Oh, Buddy, I knew you'd forgive me and recognize there was some sense to my notion."

She was mistaken. My merriment had other origins. Two. One was the picture of Uncle B. carving turkey for all those cantankerous Hendersons. The second was: It had occurred to me that I had no cause for alarm; Miss Sook might extend the invitation and Odd's mother might accept it in his behalf; but Odd wouldn't show up in a million years.

He would be too proud. For instance, throughout

the Depression years, our school distributed free milk and sandwiches to all children whose families were too poor to provide them with a lunch box. But Odd, emaciated as he was, refused to have anything to do with these handouts; he'd wander off by himself and devour a pocketful of peanuts or gnaw a large raw turnip. This kind of pride was characteristic of the Henderson breed: they might steal, gouge the gold out of a dead man's teeth, but they would never accept a gift offered openly, for anything smacking of charity was offensive to them. Odd was sure to figure Miss Sook's invitation as a charitable gesture; or see it— and not incorrectly—as a blackmailing stunt meant to make him ease up on me.

I went to bed that night with a light heart, for I was certain my Thanksgiving would not be marred by the presence of such an unsuitable visitor.

The next morning I had a bad cold, which was pleasant; it meant no school. It also meant I could have a fire in my room and cream-of-tomato soup and hours alone with Mr. Micawber and David Copperfield: the happiest of stayabeds. It was drizzling again; but true to her promise, my friend fetched her hat, a straw cartwheel decorated with weather-faded velvet roses, and set out for the Henderson home. "I won't be but a minute," she said. In fact, she was gone the better part of two hours. I couldn't imagine Miss Sook sustaining so long a conversation except with me or herself (she talked to herself often, a habit of sane persons of a solitary nature); and when she returned, she did seem drained.

Still wearing her hat and an old loose raincoat, she slipped a thermometer in my mouth, then sat at the foot of the bed. "I like her," she said firmly. "I always have liked Molly Henderson. She does all she can, and the house was clean as Bob Spencer's fingernails"— Bob Spencer being a Baptist minister famed for his hygienic gleam—"but bitter cold. With a tin roof and the wind right in the room and not a scrap of fire in the fireplace. She offered me refreshment, and I surely would have welcomed a cup of coffee, but I said no. Because I don't expect there was any coffee on the premises. Or sugar.

"It made me feel ashamed, Buddy. It hurts me all the way down to see somebody struggling like Molly. Never able to see a clear day. I don't say people should have everything they want. Though, come to think of it, I don't see what's wrong with that, either. You ought to have a bike to ride, and why shouldn't Queenie have a beef bone every day? Yes, now it's come to me, now I understand: We really all of us ought to have everything we want. I'll bet you a dime that's what the Lord intends. And when all around us we see people who can't satisfy the plainest needs, I feel ashamed. Oh, not of myself, because who am I, an old nobody who never owned a mite; if I hadn't had a family to pay my way, I'd have starved or been sent to the County Home. The shame I feel is for all of us who have anything extra when other people have nothing.

"I mentioned to Molly how we had more quilts here than we could ever use—there's a trunk of scrap quilts in the attic, the ones I made when I was a girl and couldn't go outdoors much. But she cut me off, said the Hendersons were doing just fine, thank you, and the only thing they wanted was Dad to be set free and sent home to his people. 'Miss Sook,' she told me, 'Dad is a good husband, no matter what else he might be.' Meanwhile, she has her children to care for.

"And, Buddy, you must be wrong about her boy Odd. At least partially. Molly says he's a great help to her and a great comfort. Never complains, regardless of how many chores she gives him. Says he can sing good as you hear on the radio, and when the younger children start raising a ruckus, he can quiet them down by singing to them. Bless us," she lamented, retrieving the thermometer, "all we can do for people like Molly is respect them and remember them in our prayers."

The thermometer had kept me silent; now I demanded, "But what about the invitation?"

"Sometimes," she said, scowling at the scarlet thread in the glass, "I think these eyes are giving out. At my age, a body starts to look around very closely. So you'll remember how cobwebs really looked. But to answer your question, Molly was happy to hear you thought enough of Odd to ask him over for Thanksgiving. And," she continued, ignoring my groan, "she said she was sure he'd be tickled to come. Your temperature is just over the hundred mark. I guess you can count on staying home tomorrow. That ought to bring smiles! Let's see you smile, Buddy."

As it happened, I was smiling a good deal during the next few days prior to the big feast, for my cold had advanced to croup and I was out of school the entire period. I had no contact with Odd Henderson and therefore could not personally ascertain his reaction to the invitation; but I imagined it must have made him laugh first and spit next. The prospect of his actually appearing didn't worry me; it was as farfetched a possibility as Queenie snarling at me or Miss Sook betraying my trust in her.

Yet Odd remained a presence, a redheaded silhouette on the threshold of my cheerfulness. Still, I was tantalized by the description his mother had provided; I wondered if it was true he had another side, that somewhere underneath the evil a speck of humaneness existed. But that was impossible! Anybody who believed so would leave their house unlocked when the gypsies came to town. All you had to do was look at him.

Miss Sook was aware that my croup was not as severe as I pretended, and so in the mornings, when the others had absented themselves—Uncle B. to his farms and the sisters to their dry-goods store—she tolerated my getting out of bed and even let me assist in the springlike house-cleaning that always preceded the Thanksgiving assembly. There was such a lot to do, enough for a dozen hands. We polished the parlor furniture, the piano, the black curio cabinet (which contained only a fragment of Stone Mountain the sisters had brought back from a business trip to Atlanta), the formal walnut rockers and florid Biedermeier pieces—rubbed them with lemon-scented wax until the place was shiny as lemon skin and smelled like a citrus grove. Curtains were laundered and rehung, pillows punched, rugs beaten; wherever one glanced, dust motes and tiny feathers drifted in the sparkling November light sifting through the tall rooms. Poor Queenie was relegated to the kitchen, for fear she might leave a stray hair, perhaps a flea, in the more dignified areas of the house.

The most delicate task was preparing the napkins and tablecloths that would decorate the dining room. The linen had belonged to my friend's mother, who had received it as a wedding gift; though it had been used only once or twice a year, say two hundred times in the past eighty years, nevertheless it was eighty years old, and mended patches and freckled discolorations were apparent. Probably it had not been a fine material to begin with, but Miss Sook treated it as though it had been woven by golden hands on heavenly looms: "My mother said, 'The day may come when all we can offer is well water and cold cornbread, but at least we'll be able to serve it on a table set with proper linen.'"

At night, after the day's dashing about and when the rest of the house was dark, one feeble lamp burned late while my friend, propped in bed with napkins massed on her lap, repaired blemishes and tears with thread and needle, her forehead crumpled, her eyes cruelly squeezed, yet illuminated by the fatigued rapture of a pilgrim approaching an altar at journey's end.

From hour to hour, as the shivery tolls of the faraway courthouse clock numbered ten and eleven and twelve, I would wake up and see her lamp still lit, and would drowsily lurch into her room to reprimand her: "You ought to be asleep!"

"In a minute, Buddy. I can't just now. When I think of all the company coming, it scares me. Starts my head whirling," she said, ceasing to stitch and rubbing her eyes. "Whirling with stars."

Chrysanthemums: some as big as a baby's head. Bundles of curled penny-colored leaves with flickering lavender underhues. "Chrysanthemums," my friend commented as we moved through our garden stalking flower-show blossoms with decapitating shears, "are like lions. Kingly characters. I always expect them to *spring*. To turn on me with a growl and a roar."

It was the kind of remark that caused people to wonder about Miss Sook, though I understand that only in retrospect, for I always knew just what she meant, and in this instance the whole idea of it, the notion of lugging all those growling gorgeous roaring lions into the house and caging them in tacky vases (our final decorative act on Thanksgiving Eve) made us so giggly and giddy and stupid we were soon out of breath.

"Look at Queenie," my friend said, stuttering with mirth. "Look at her ears, Buddy. Standing straight up. She's thinking, Well, what kind of lunatics are these I'm mixed up with? Ah, Queenie. Come here, honey. I'm going to give you a biscuit dipped in hot coffee."

A lively day, that Thanksgiving. Lively with on-and-off showers and abrupt sky clearings accompanied by thrusts of raw sun and sudden bandit winds snatching autumn's leftover leaves.

The noises of the house were lovely, too: pots and pans and Uncle B.'s unused and rusty voice as he stood in the hall in his creaking Sunday suit, greeting our guests as they arrived. A few came by horseback or mule-drawn wagon, the majority in shined-up farm trucks and rackety flivvers. Mr. and Mrs. Conklin and their four beautiful daughters drove up in a mint-green 1932 Chevrolet (Mr. Conklin was well off; he owned several fishing smackers that operated out of Mobile), an object which aroused warm curiosity among the men present; they studied and poked it and all but took it apart.

The first guests to arrive were Mrs. Mary Taylor Wheelwright, escorted by her custodians, a grandson and his wife. She was a pretty little thing, Mrs. Wheelwright; she wore her age as lightly as the tiny red bonnet that, like the cherry on a vanilla sundae, sat perkily atop her milky hair. "Darlin' Bobby," she said, hugging Uncle B., "I realize we're an itty-bit early, but you know me, always punctual to a fault." Which was an apology deserved, for it was not yet nine o'clock and guests weren't expected much before noon.

However, everybody arrived earlier than we intended—except the Perk McCloud family, who suffered two blowouts in the space of thirty miles and arrived in such a stomping temper, particularly Mr. McCloud, that we feared for the china. Most of these people lived year-round in lonesome places hard to get away from: isolated farms, whistle-stops and crossroads, empty river hamlets or lumber-camp communities deep in the pine forests; so of course it was eagerness that caused them to be early, primed for an affectionate and memorable gathering.

And so it was. Some while ago, I had a letter from one of the Conklin sisters, now the wife of a naval captain and living in San Diego; she wrote: "I think of you often around this time of year, I suppose because of what happened at one of our Alabama Thanksgivings. It was a few years before Miss Sook died—would it be 1933? Golly, I'll never forget that day."

By noon, not another soul could be accommodated in the parlor, a hive humming with women's tattle and womanly aromas: Mrs. Wheelwright smelled of lilac water and Annabel Conklin like geraniums after rain. The odor of tobacco fanned out across the porch, where most of the men had clustered, despite the wavering weather, the alternations between sprinkles of rain and sunlit wind squalls. Tobacco was a substance alien to the setting; true, Miss Sook now and again secretly dipped snuff, a taste acquired under unknown tutelage and one she refused to discuss; her sisters would have been mortified had they suspected, and Uncle B., too, for he took a harsh stand on all stimulants, condemning them morally and medically.

The virile redolence of cigars, the pungent nip of pipe smoke, the tortoiseshell richness they evoked, constantly lured me out of the parlor onto the porch, though it was the parlor I preferred, due to the presence of the Conklin sisters, who played by turn our untuned piano with a gifted, rollicking lack of airs. "Indian Love Call" was among their repertoire, and also a 1918 war ballad, the lament of a child pleading with a house thief, entitled "Don't Steal Daddy's Medals, He Won Them for Bravery." Annabel played and sang it; she was the oldest of the sisters and the loveliest, though it was a chore to pick among them, for they were like quadruplets of unequal height. One thought of apples, compact and flavorful, sweet but cider-tart; their hair, loosely plaited, had the blue luster of a well-groomed ebony racehorse, and certain features, eyebrows, noses, lips when smiling, tilted in an original style that added humor to their charms. The nicest thing was that they were a bit plump: "pleasingly plump" describes it precisely.

It was while listening to Annabel at the piano, and falling in love with her, that I felt Odd Henderson. I say *felt* because I was aware of him before I saw him: the sense of peril that warns, say, an experienced woodsman of an impending encounter with a rattler or bobcat alerted me.

I turned, and there the fellow stood at the parlor entrance, half in, half out. To others he must have seemed simply a grubby twelve-year-old beanpole who had made some attempt to rise to the event by parting and slicking his difficult hair, the comb grooves were still damply intact. But to me he was as unexpected and sinister as a genie released from a bottle. What a dumbhead I'd been to think he wouldn't show up! Only a dunce wouldn't have guessed that he would come out of spite: the joy of spoiling for me this awaited day.

However, Odd had not yet seen me: Annabel, her firm, acrobatic fingers somersaulting over the warped piano keys, had diverted him, for he was watching her, lips separated, eyes slitted, as though he had come upon her disrobed and cooling herself in the local river. It was as if he were contemplating some wished-for vision; his already red ears had become pimiento. The entrancing scene so dazed him I was able to squeeze directly past him and run along the hall to the kitchen. "He's here!"

My friend had completed her work hours earlier; moreover she had two colored women helping out. Nevertheless she had been hiding in the kitchen since our party started, under a pretense of keeping the exiled Queenie company. In truth, she was afraid of mingling with any group, even one composed of relatives, which was why, despite her reliance on the Bible and its Hero, she rarely went to church. Although she loved all children and was at ease with them, she was not acceptable as a child, yet she could not accept herself as a peer of grownups and in a collection of them behaved like an awkward young lady, silent and rather astonished. But the *idea* of parties exhilarated her; what a pity she couldn't take part invisibly, for then how festive she would have felt.

I noticed that my friend's hands were trembling; so were mine. Her usual outfit consisted of calico dresses, tennis shoes and Uncle B.'s discarded sweaters; she had no clothes appropriate to starchy occasions. Today she was lost inside something borrowed from one of her stout sisters, a creepy navy-blue dress its owner had worn to every funeral in the county since time remembered.

"He's here," I informed her for the third time. "Odd Henderson."

"Then why aren't you with him?" she said admonishingly. "That's not polite, Buddy. He's your particular guest. You ought to be out there seeing he meets everybody and has a good time."

"I *can't*. I can't speak to him."

Queenie was curled on her lap, having a head rub; my friend stood up, dumping Queenie and disclosing a stretch of navy-blue material sprinkled with dog hair, said "*Buddy*. You mean you haven't spoken to that boy!" My rudeness obliterated her timidity; taking me by the hand, she steered me to the parlor.

She need not have fretted over Odd's welfare. The charms of Annabel Conklin had drawn him to the piano. Indeed, he was scrunched up beside her on the piano seat, sitting there studying her delightful profile, his eyes opaque as the orbs of the stuffed whale I'd seen that summer when a touring honky-tonk passed through town (it was advertised as *The Original Moby Dick,* and it cost five cents to view the remains—what a bunch of crooks!). As for Annabel, she would flirt with anything that walked or crawled—no, that's unfair, for it was really a form of generosity, of simply being alive. Still, it gave me a hurt to see her playing cute with that mule skinner.

Hauling me onward, my friend introduced herself to him: "Buddy and I, we're so happy you could come." Odd had the manners of a billy goat: he didn't stand up or offer his hand, hardly looked at her and at me not at all. Daunted but dead game, my friend said: "Maybe Odd will sing us a tune. I know he can; his mother told me so. Annabel, sugar, play something Odd can sing."

Reading back, I see that I haven't thoroughly described Odd Henderson's ears—a major omission, for they were a pair of eye-catchers, like Alfalfa's in the *Our Gang* comedy pictures. Now, because of Annabel's flattering receptivity to my friend's request, his ears became so beet-bright it made your eyes smart. He mumbled, he shook his head hangdog; but Annabel said: "Do you know 'I Have Seen the Light'?" He didn't, but her next suggestion was greeted with a grin of recognition; the biggest fool could tell his modesty was all put on.

Giggling, Annabel struck a rich chord, and Odd, in a voice precociously manly, sang: "When the red, red robin comes bob, bob, bobbin' along." The Adam's apple in his tense throat jumped; Annabel's enthusiasm accelerated; the women's shrill hen chatter slackened as they became aware of the entertainment. Odd was good, he could sing for sure, and the jealousy charging through me had enough power to electrocute a murderer. Murder was what I had in mind; I could have killed him as easily as swat a mosquito. Easier.

Once more, unnoticed even by my friend, who was absorbed in the musicale, I escaped the parlor and sought The Island. That was the name I had given a place in the house where I went when I felt blue or inexplicably exuberant or just when I wanted to think things over. It was a mammoth closet attached to our only bathroom; the bathroom itself, except for its sanitary fixtures, was like a cozy winter parlor, with a horsehair love seat, scatter rugs, a bureau, a fireplace and framed reproductions of "The Doctor's Visit," "September Morn," "The Swan Pool" and calendars galore.

There were two small stained-glass windows in the closet; lozenge-like patterns of rose, amber and green light filtered through the windows, which looked out on the bathroom proper. Here and there patches of color had faded from the glass or been chipped away; by applying an eye to one of these clearings, it was possible to identify the room's visitors. After I'd been secluded there awhile, brooding over my enemy's success, footsteps intruded: Mrs. Mary Taylor Wheelwright, who stopped before a mirror, smacked her face with a powder puff, rouged her antique cheeks and then, perusing the effect, announced: "Very nice, Mary. Even if Mary says so herself."

It is well known that women outlive men; could it merely be superior vanity that keeps them going? Anyway, Mrs. Wheelwright sweetened my mood, so when, following her departure, a heartily rung dinner bell sounded through the house, I decided to quit my refuge and enjoy the feast, regardless of Odd Henderson.

But just then footsteps echoed again. *He* appeared, looking less sullen than I'd ever seen him. Strutty. Whistling. Unbuttoning his trousers and letting go with a forceful splash, he whistled along, jaunty as a jaybird in a field of sunflowers. As he was leaving, an open box on the bureau summoned his attention. It was a cigar box in which my friend kept recipes torn out of newspapers and other junk, as well as a cameo brooch her father had long ago given her. Sentimental value aside, her imagination had conferred upon the object a rare costliness; whenever we had cause for serious grievance against her sisters or Uncle B., she would say, "Never mind, Buddy. We'll sell my cameo and go away. We'll take the bus to New Orleans." Though never discussing what we would do once we arrived in New Orleans, or what we would live on after the cameo money ran out, we both relished this fantasy. Perhaps each of us secretly realized the brooch was only a Sears Roebuck novelty; all the same, it seemed to us a talisman of true, though untested, magic: a charm that promised us our freedom if indeed we did decide to pursue our luck in fabled spheres. So my friend never wore it, for it was too much a treasure to risk its loss or damage.

Now I saw Odd's sacrilegious fingers reach toward it, watched him bounce it in the palm of his hand, drop it back in the box and turn to go. Then return. This time he swiftly retrieved the cameo and sneaked it into his pocket. My boiling first instinct was to rush out of the closet and challenge him; at that moment, I believe I could have pinned Odd to the floor. *But—* Well, do you recall how, in simpler days, funny-paper artists used to illustrate the birth of an idea by sketching an incandescent light bulb above the brow of Mutt or Jeff or whomever? That's how it was with me: a sizzling light bulb suddenly radiated my brain. The shock and brilliance of it made me burn and shiver—laugh, too. Odd had handed me an ideal instrument for revenge, one that would make up for all the cockleburs.

In the dining room, long tables had been joined to shape a T. Uncle B. was at the upper center, Mrs. Mary Taylor Wheelwright at his right and Mrs. Conklin at his left. Odd was seated between two of the Conklin sisters, one of them Annabel, whose compliments kept him in top condition. My friend had put herself at the foot of the table among the youngest children; according to her, she had chosen the position because it provided quicker access to the kitchen, but of course it was because that was where she wished to be. Queenie, who had somehow got loose, was under the table—trembling and wagging with ecstasy as she skittered between the rows of legs—but nobody seemed to object, probably because they were hypnotized by the uncarved, lusciously glazed turkeys and the excellent aromas rising from dishes of okra and corn, onion fritters and hot mince pies.

My own mouth would have watered if it hadn't gone bone-dry at the heart-pounding prospect of total revenge. For a second, glancing at Odd Henderson's suffused face, I experienced a fragmentary regret, but I really had no qualms.

Uncle B. recited grace. Head bowed, eyes shut, calloused hands prayerfully placed, he intoned: "Bless You, O Lord, for the bounty of our table, the varied fruits we can be thankful for on this Thanksgiving Day of a troubled year"—his voice, so infrequently heard, croaked with the hollow imperfections of an old organ in an abandoned church—"Amen."

Then, as chairs were adjusted and napkins rustled, the necessary pause I'd been listening for arrived. "Someone here is a thief." I spoke clearly and repeated the accusation in even more measured tones: "Odd Henderson is a thief. He stole Miss Sook's cameo."

Napkins gleamed in suspended, immobilized hands. Men coughed, the Conklin sisters gasped in quadruplet unison and little Perk McCloud, Jr., began to hiccup, as very young children will when startled.

My friend, in a voice teetering between reproach

and anguish, said, "Buddy doesn't mean that. He's only teasing."

"I do mean it. If you don't believe me, go look in your box. The cameo isn't there. Odd Henderson has it in his pocket."

"Buddy's had a bad croup," she murmured. "Don't blame him, Odd. He hasn't a notion what he's saying."

I said, "Go look in your box. I saw him take it."

Uncle B., staring at me with an alarming wintriness, took charge. "Maybe you'd better," he told Miss Sook. "That should settle the matter."

It was not often that my friend disobeyed her brother; she did not now. But her pallor, the mortified angle of her shoulders, revealed with what distaste she accepted the errand. She was gone only a minute, but her absence seemed an eon. Hostility sprouted and surged around the table like a thorn-encrusted vine growing with uncanny speed—and the victim trapped in its tendrils was not the accused, but his accuser. Stomach sickness gripped me; Odd, on the other hand, seemed calm as a corpse.

Miss Sook returned, smiling. "Shame on you, Buddy," she chided, shaking a finger. "Playing that kind of joke. My cameo was exactly where I left it."

Uncle B. said, "Buddy, I want to hear you apologize to our guest."

"No, he don't have to do that," Odd Henderson said, rising. "He was telling the truth." He dug into his pocket and put the cameo on the table. "I wish I had some excuse to give. But I ain't got none." Starting for the door, he said, "You must be a special lady, Miss Sook, to fib for me like that." And then, damn his soul, he walked right out of there.

So did I. Except I ran. I pushed back my chair, knocking it over. The crash triggered Queenie; she scooted from under the table, barked and bared her teeth. And Miss Sook, as I went past her, tried to stop me: "Buddy!" But I wanted no part of her or Queenie. That dog had snarled at me and my friend had taken Odd Henderson's side, she'd lied to save his skin, betrayed our friendship, my love: things I'd thought could never happen.

Simpson's pasture lay below the house, a meadow brilliant with high November gold and russet grass. At the edge of the pasture there were a gray barn, a pig corral, a fenced-in chicken yard and a smokehouse. It was the smokehouse I slipped into, a black chamber cool on even the hottest summer days. It had a dirt floor and a smoke pit that smelled of hickory cinders and creosote; rows of hams hung from rafters. It was a place I'd always been wary of, but now its darkness seemed sheltering. I fell on the ground, my ribs heaving like the gills of a beach-stranded fish; and I didn't care that I was demolishing my one nice suit, the one with long trousers, by thrashing about on the floor in a messy mixture of earth and ashes and pork grease.

One thing I knew: I was going to quit that house, that town, that night. Hit the road. Hop a freight and head for California. Make my living shining shoes in Hollywood. Fred Astaire's shoes. Clark Gable's. Or— maybe I just might become a movie star myself. Look at Jackie Cooper. Oh, they'd be sorry then. When I was rich and famous and refused to answer their letters and even telegrams, probably.

Suddenly I thought of something that would make them even sorrier. The door to the shed was ajar, and a knife of sunshine exposed a shelf supporting several bottles. Dusty bottles with skull-and-crossbone labels. If I drank from one of those, then all of them up there in the dining room, the whole swilling and gobbling caboodle, would know what sorry was. It was worth it, if only to witness Uncle B.'s remorse when they found me cold and stiff on the smokehouse floor; worth it to hear the human wails and Queenie's howls as my coffin was lowered into cemetery depths.

The only hitch was, I wouldn't actually be able to see or hear any of this: how could I, being dead? And unless one can observe the guilt and regret of the mourners, surely there is nothing satisfactory about being dead?

Uncle B. must have forbidden Miss Sook to go look for me until the last guest had left the table. It was late afternoon before I heard her voice floating across the pasture; she called my name softly, forlornly as a mourning dove. I stayed where I was and did not answer.

It was Queenie who found me; she came sniffing around the smokehouse and yapped when she caught my scent, then entered and crawled toward me and licked my hand, an ear and a cheek; she knew she had treated me badly.

Presently, the door swung open and the light widened. My friend said, "Come here, Buddy." And I wanted to go to her. When she saw me, she laughed. "Goodness, boy. You look dipped in tar and all ready for feathering." But there were no recriminations or references to my ruined suit.

Queenie trotted off to pester some cows; and trailing after her into the pasture, we sat down on a tree stump. "I saved you a drumstick," she said, handing me a parcel wrapped in waxed paper. "And your favorite piece of turkey. The pulley."

The hunger that direr sensations had numbed now hit me like a belly-punch. I gnawed the drumstick clean, then stripped the pulley, the sweet part of the turkey around the wishbone.

While I was eating, Miss Sook put her arm around my shoulders. "There's just this I want to say, Buddy.

Two wrongs never made a right. It was wrong of him to take the cameo. But we don't know why he took it. Maybe he never meant to keep it. Whatever his reason, it can't have been calculated. Which is why what you did was much worse: you *planned* to humiliate him. It was deliberate. Now listen to me, Buddy: there is only one unpardonable sin—*deliberate cruelty*. All else can be forgiven. That, never. Do you understand me, Buddy?"

I did, dimly, and time has taught me that she was right. But at that moment I mainly comprehended that because my revenge had failed, my method must have been wrong. Odd Henderson had emerged—how? why?—as someone superior to me, even more honest.

"Do you, Buddy? Understand?"

"Sort of. Pull," I said, offering her one prong of the wishbone.

We split it; my half was the larger, which entitled me to a wish. She wanted to know what I'd wished.

"That you're still my friend."

"Dumbhead," she said, and hugged me.

"Forever?"

"I won't be here forever, Buddy. Nor will you." Her voice sank like the sun on the pasture's horizon, was silent a second and then climbed with the strength of a new sun. "But yes, forever. The Lord willing, you'll be here long after I've gone. And as long as you remember me, then we'll always be together." . . .

Afterward, Odd Henderson let me alone. He started tussling with a boy his own age, Squirrel McMillan. And the next year, because of Odd's poor grades and general bad conduct, our school principal wouldn't allow him to attend classes, so he spent the winter working as a hand on a dairy farm. The last time I saw him was shortly before he hitchhiked to Mobile, joined the Merchant Marine and disappeared. It must have been the year before I was packed off to a miserable fate in a military academy, and two years prior to my friend's death. That would make it the autumn of 1934.

Miss Sook had summoned me to the garden; she had transplanted a blossoming chrysanthemum bush into a tin washtub and needed help to haul it up the steps onto the front porch, where it would make a fine display. It was heavier than forty fat pirates, and while we were struggling with it ineffectually, Odd Henderson passed along the road. He paused at the garden gate and then opened it, saying, "Let me do that for you, ma'am." Life on a dairy farm had done him a lot of good; he'd thickened, his arms were sinewy and his red coloring had deepened to a ruddy brown. Airily he lifted the big tub and placed it on the porch.

My friend said, "I'm obliged to you, sir. That was neighborly."

"Nothing," he said, still ignoring me.

Miss Sook snapped the stems of her showiest blooms. "Take these to your mother," she told him, handing him the bouquet. "And give her my love."

"Thank you, ma'am. I will."

"Oh, Odd," she called, after he'd regained the road, "be careful! They're lions, you know." But he was already out of hearing. We watched until he turned a bend at the corner, innocent of the menace he carried, the chrysanthemums that burned, that growled and roared against a greenly lowering dusk.

The Hidden Songs of a Secret Soul

by Bob Greene

Are there any people in your life who remind you of Boo Radley? The following essay is a modern-day song of the self, a profile of a person with a surprising, and secret, leisure-time pursuit.

Lenny was the loneliest of dreamers. No one knew; we wouldn't have known, either, except for the fact that the afternoons got long, and the only way to make it through was to talk. After a time we even talked to Lenny.

He worked in the shipping room of a bottling plant. It manufactured soda pop. Lenny was a thin, slight man in his middle forties with a stammer and a sad face. We worked at long tables. Lenny was the only full-timer at our table; the rest of us were in school, and we came in whatever afternoons we could spare and picked up pocket money for the weekends. For us, the job was a dreary way to kill time. For Lenny, it was his sustenance.

The other full-timers in the room liked to kid Lenny. Most of them were in their twenties, and they passed the day with talk of women and late-night intrigue. Lenny had no wife or family, and he never spoke of a woman. So when the full-timers became bored with their own talk, they would call over to our table and rag Lenny some. They would ask him about his romances, and when he would become embarrassed and turn away and try not to answer, they would not let up until they became bored with bothering him. They didn't mean anything by it.

He never said much, and for awhile we didn't say

much to him. We would come in after classes, nod hello to him, and start loading boxes. Lenny had spent most of his life being invisible; we sensed that without really thinking about it. He just seemed happy that we didn't rag him like the others did.

One afternoon, though, he started to talk. He didn't slow up what he was doing, but as he worked he began to ask us about the classes we took in school, the courses we were studying. He asked if any of us were studying English as a major; he wanted to know if any of us were studying the great poets.

None of us thought much about the questions at first; I know I didn't. But after that, a couple of times every week, he would ask the same things. It was always about the poets. On the way back home in the evenings, we would talk about it and wonder what he meant. One night we determined that we would find out.

So the next day, at break time, we asked Lenny to sit down for coffee with us. We had never had coffee with Lenny before; usually he would disappear on his break. One of us asked him about the poets.

"I just wondered," Lenny said. But we pressed.

He avoided it, and so we dropped it and finished our cups. Just before we were due back at our table, Lenny said, "Sometimes I write poems."

We went back to work and tried to make him tell us more. It was so unlikely, the idea of Lenny, who seldom had the nerve to speak and had trouble when he did, spending time committing his thoughts to paper. When we attempted to question him further, he became uncomfortable and flushed.

"Don't talk so loud," he pleaded. "The others will hear."

We asked him that day if he would let us see his poems, and he said no. We kept it up, though; we wanted to see. Finally he said that he would like to let us see them but that he was afraid that if he brought them in, the others would find out and make fun of him.

We told him we would go with him to see the poems. He said he would think about it, and we did not let him forget. One day he said that we could come home with him if we wished.

After work we rode the el. He lived in one room. There were not enough places for us to sit. He brought out a large scrapbook. The poems were inside.

They were written all in longhand, with a fountain pen. Even before we started to read them, they looked elegant. Lenny's hand moved with strokes full of flourish and style, confident and strong, while Lenny was timid and quiet. And when we did begin to read, the poems were beautiful. The verses were long, and rich with imagery and detail. They told of love, and of spiritual triumphs, and of life in faraway places. They were music. We must have sat and read for an hour, saying nothing. When we finished and looked up, there was Lenny, in his rented room, staring away from us.

"Please never say anything to the others," he said.

We tried to tell him how good the poems were, how he should be proud of what he had done, and not ashamed to let anyone know, but he cut us off.

"Please," he said. "I have to work there."

We went home, and the next day Lenny let us know, without a word, that we were not to talk about the poems again. For a few months we continued to work, and Lenny continued to take the joking from the other full-timers. Then school ended for the summer, and we left the job, and Lenny. We never went back.

The reason I am thinking about this is that I saw him the other day. There was no mistake; it was he. It was on a crowded street, and there was Lenny. I motioned to him, and called his name, and started walking toward him. He saw me; I know he did. He turned around very quickly and walked away, and I knew that I was not supposed to follow.

Freedom

by Langston Hughes

Like Tom Robinson, the speaker of
Hughes's poem wants to experience the
power of freedom now, in the present.

Freedom will not come
Today, this year
   Nor ever
Through compromise and fear.

5   I have as much right
As the other fellow has
   To stand
On my two feet
And own the land.

10   I tire so of hearing people say,
Let things take their course.
Tomorrow is another day.
I do not need my freedom when I'm dead.
I cannot live on tomorrow's bread.
15   Freedom
     Is a strong seed
     Planted
     In a great need.
     I live here, too.
20   I want freedom
     Just as you.

You Wouldn't Understand

by José Emilio Pacheco

What would you do if you witnessed an injustice? How would you explain your actions (or lack thereof) to another person?

She took my hand as we crossed the street, and I felt the dampness of her palm.

"I want to play in the park for a while."

"No. It's too late. We have to get home; your mother is waiting for us. Look, there's nobody else around. All the little children are home in bed."

The streetlight changed. The cars moved forward. We ran across the street. The smell of exhaust dissolved into the freshness of grass and foliage. The last remnants of rain evaporated or were absorbed by the sprouts, leaves, roots, nervations.

"Are there going to be any mushrooms?"

"Yes, I guess so."

"When?"

"Well, I guess by tomorrow there should be some."

"Will you bring me here to see them?"

"Yes, but you'll have to go to bed right away so you can get up early."

I walked too quickly, and the child had to hurry to keep up with me. She stopped, lifted her eyes, looked at me to gain courage, and asked, slightly embarrassed, "Daddy, do dwarfs really exist?"

"Well, they do in stories."

"And witches?"

"Yes, but also just in stories."

"That's not true."

"Why?"

"I've seen witches on TV, and they scare me a lot."

"They shouldn't. Everything you see on television is also stories—with witches—made up to entertain children, not scare them."

"Oh, so everything they show on TV is just stories?"

"No, not everything. I mean . . . how can I explain it to you? You wouldn't understand."

Night fell. A livid firmament fluted with grayish clouds. In the garbage cans, Sunday's refuse began to decay: newspapers, beer cans, sandwich wrappers. Beyond the distant drone of traffic, raindrops could be heard falling from the leaves and tree trunks onto the grass. The path wound through a clearing between two groves of trees. At that moment, the shouts reached my ears: ten or twelve boys had surrounded another. With his back against the tree, he looked at them with fear but did not scream for help or mercy.

My daughter grabbed my hand again.

"What are they doing?"

"I don't know. Fighting. Let's go. Come on, hurry up."

The fragile pressure of her fingers was like a reproach. She had figured it out: I was accountable to her. At the same time, my daughter represented an alibi, a defense against fear and excessive guilt.

We stood absolutely still. I managed to see the face—the dark skin reddened by white hands—of the boy who was being festively beaten by the others. I shouted at them to stop. Only one of them turned around to look at me, and he made a threatening, scornful gesture. The girl watched all of this without blinking. The boy fell, and they kicked him on the ground. Someone picked him up, and the others kept slugging him. I did not dare move. I wanted to believe that if I did not intervene, it was to protect my daughter, because I knew there was nothing I could do against all twelve of them.

"Daddy, tell them to stop. Scold them."

"Don't move. Wait here for me."

Before I finished speaking, they were already running quickly away, dispersing in all directions. I felt obscenely liberated. I cherished the cowardly hope that my daughter would think they had run away from me. We approached. The boy rose with difficulty. He was bleeding from his nose and mouth.

"Let me help you. I'll take you . . ."

He looked at me without answering. He wiped the blood off with the cuffs of his checkered shirt. I offered him a handkerchief. Not even a no: disgust in his eyes. Something—an undefinable horror—in the girl's expression. Both of their faces were an aura of deceit, a pain of betrayal.

He turned his back on us. He walked away dragging his feet. For a moment I thought he would collapse. He continued until he disappeared among the trees. Silence.

"Let's go. Let's get out of here."

"Why did they do that to him if he wasn't doing anything to them?"

"I guess because they were fighting."

"But there were lots of them."

"I know. I know."

"They're bad because they hit him, right?"

"Of course. That's the wrong thing to do."

The park seemed to go on forever. We would never reach the bus. We would never return home. She would never stop asking me questions nor I giving her the same answers they undoubtedly gave me at her age.

"So, that means he's good?"

"Who?"

"The boy the others made bleed?"

"Yes, I mean, I don't know."

"Or is he bad too?"

"No, no. The others are the bad ones because of what they did."

Finally we found a policeman. I described to him what I had just witnessed.

"There's nothing to be done. It happens every night. You did the right thing by not interfering. They are always armed and can be dangerous. They claim the park is only for whites and that any dirty nigger who steps foot in here will suffer the consequences."

"But they don't have the right, they can't do that."

"What are you talking about? That's what the people in the neighborhood say. But when it comes down to it, they won't let blacks come to their houses or sit in their bars."

He gave the child an affectionate pat and continued on his way. I understood that clichés like "the world's indifference" were not totally meaningless. Three human beings—the victim, my daughter, myself—had just been dramatically affected by something about which nobody else seemed to care.

I was cold, tired, and felt like closing my eyes. We reached the edge of the park. Three black boys crossed the street with us. No one had ever looked at me like that. I saw their switchblades and thought they were going to attack us. But they kept going and disappeared into the grove.

"Daddy, what are they going to do?"

"Not let happen to them what happened to the other one."

"But why do they always have to fight?"

"I can't explain it to you, it's too difficult, you wouldn't understand."

I knelt down to button up her coat. I hugged her gently, with tenderness and fear. The dampness of the trees encircled us. The park was advancing upon the city and again—or overtly—everything would be jungle.

Acknowledgments

(continued from page ii)

Random House, Inc.: "The Thanksgiving Visitor," from *The Thanksgiving Visitor* by Truman Capote; Copyright © 1967 by Truman Capote. Reprinted by permission of Random House, Inc.

Tribune Media Services: "The Hidden Songs of a Secret Soul" by Bob Greene, from the *Chicago Tribune*, March 3, 1975. Reprinted by permission of Tribune Media Services.

Alfred A. Knopf, Inc.: "Freedom," from *The Panther and the Lash* by Langston Hughes; Copyright © 1967 by Arna Bontemps and George Houston Bass. Reprinted by permission of Alfred A. Knopf, Inc.

New Directions Publishing Corporation: "You Wouldn't Understand," from *Battles in the Desert and Other Stories* by José Emilio Pacheco; Copyright © 1963, 1981 by Ediciones Era, S.A. Reprinted by permission of New Directions Publishing Corporation.